FOR ORGANS, PIANOS & ELECTRONIC KEYBOARDS

E-Z PLAY TODAY

113

COUNTRY GO

T0034080

ISBN 978-0-634-02254-8

HAL•LEONARD®
CORPORATION
7777 W. BLUEMOUND RD. P.O. BOX 13819 MILWAUKEE, WI 53213

An American Trilogy

Registration 4
Rhythm: Ballad or Country

Words and Music by
Mickey Newbury

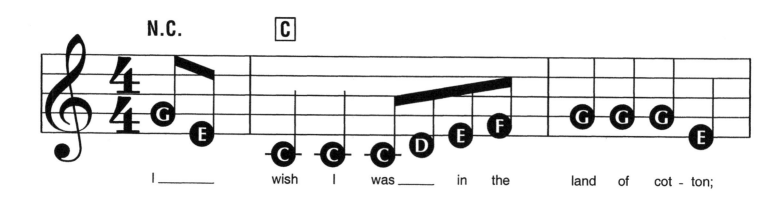

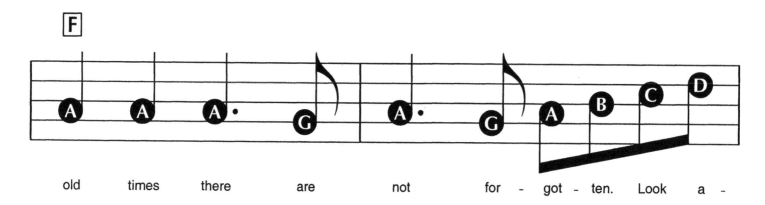

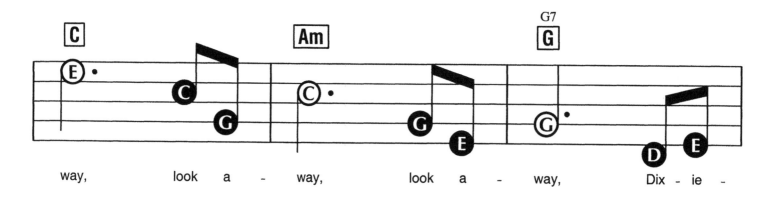

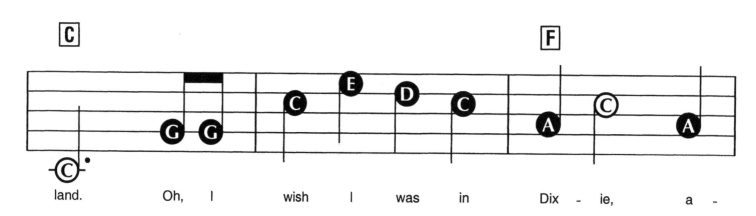

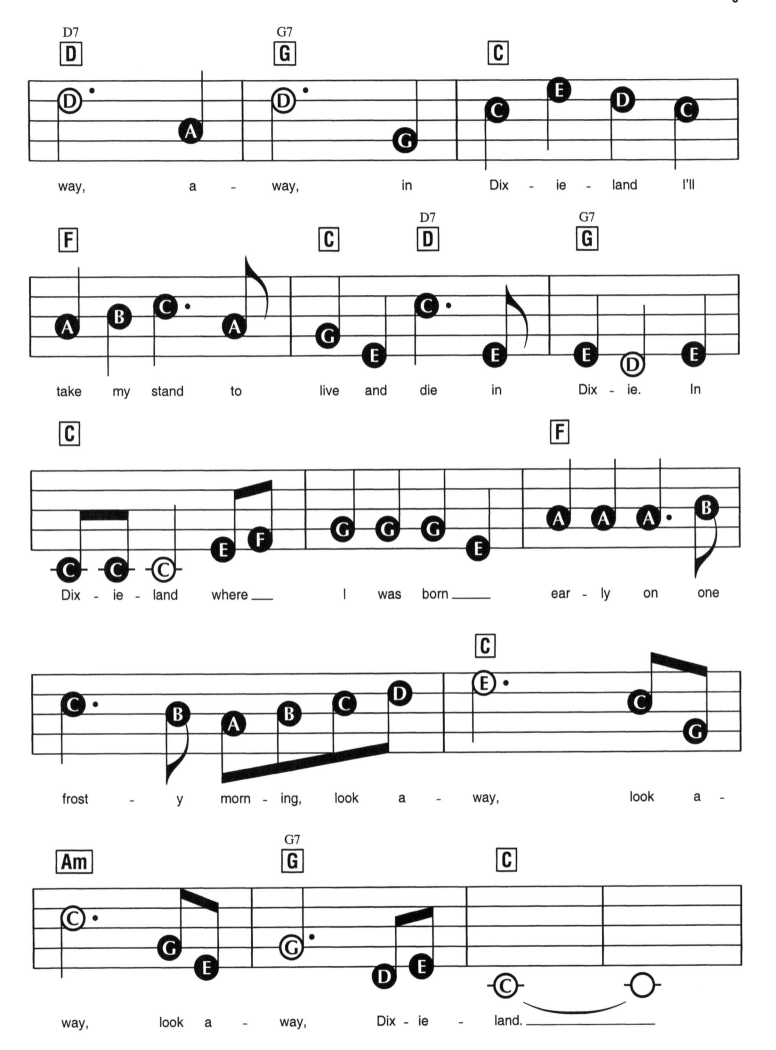

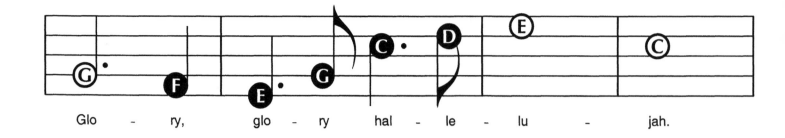

Glo - ry, glo - ry hal - le - lu - jah.

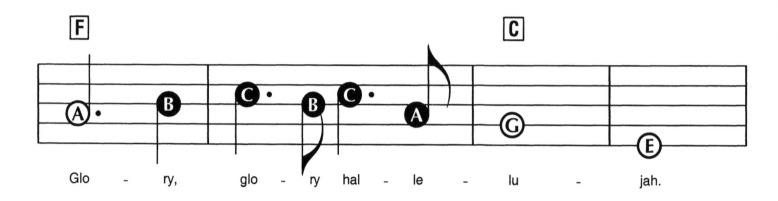

Glo - ry, glo - ry hal - le - lu - jah.

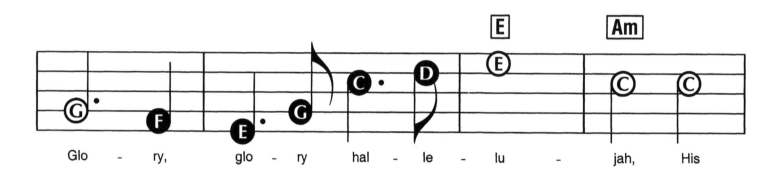

Glo - ry, glo - ry hal - le - lu - jah, His

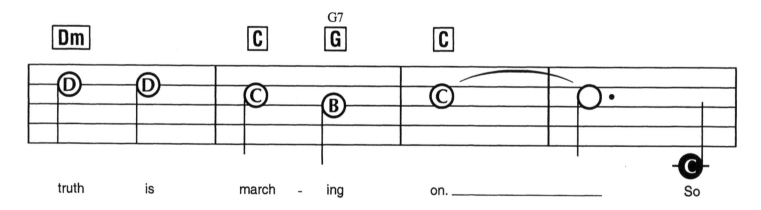

truth is march - ing on. _____ So

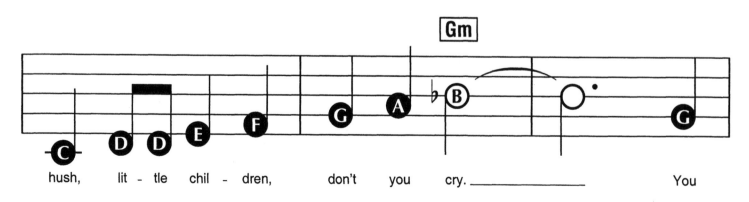

hush, lit - tle chil - dren, don't you cry. _____ You

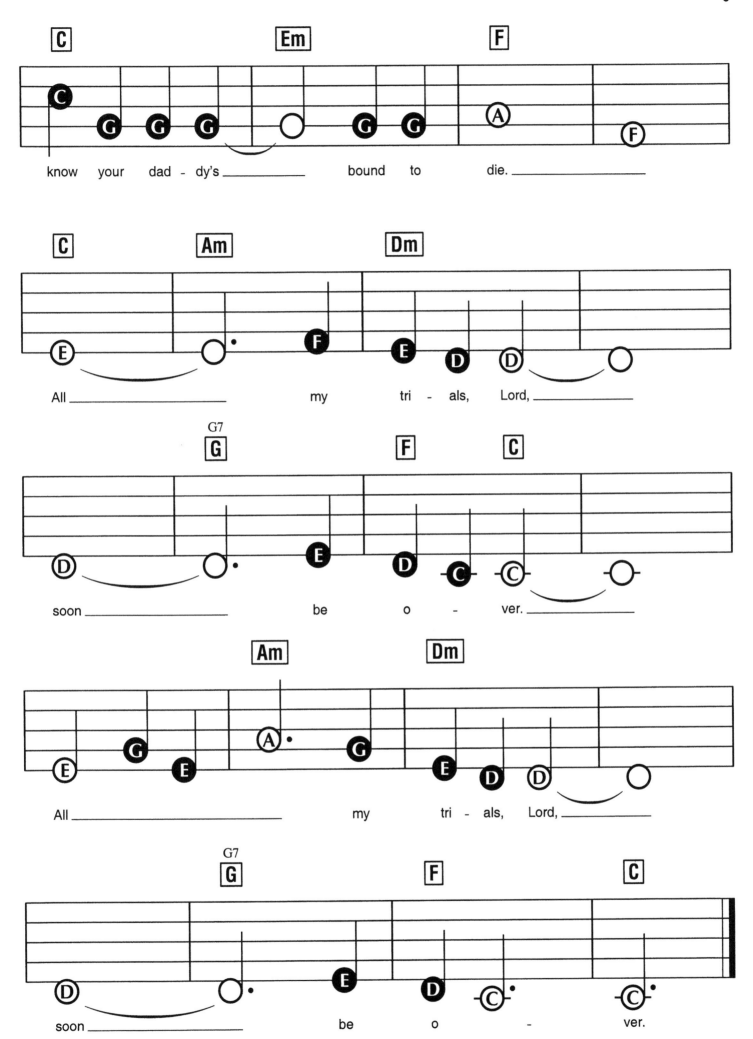

The Eastern Gate

Registration 3
Rhythm: Fox Trot or Country

Words and Music by
Isaiah G. Martin

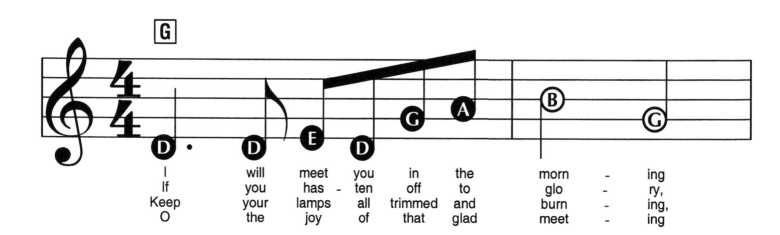

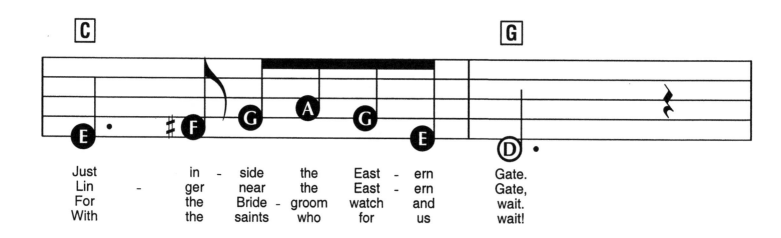

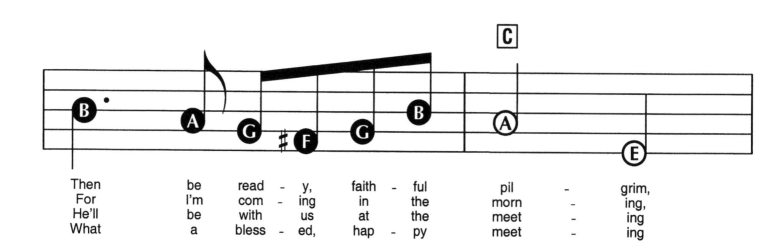

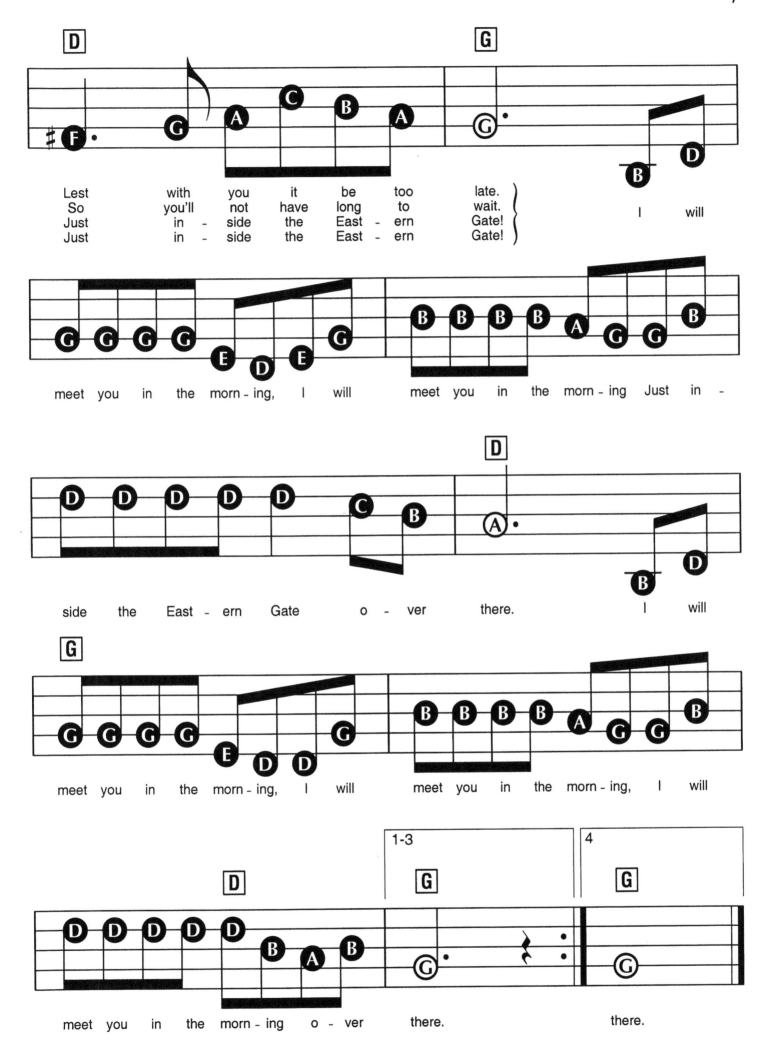

Everybody Will Be Happy Over There

Registration 9
Rhythm: Fox Trot or Country

Words and Music by
E.M. Bartlett

9

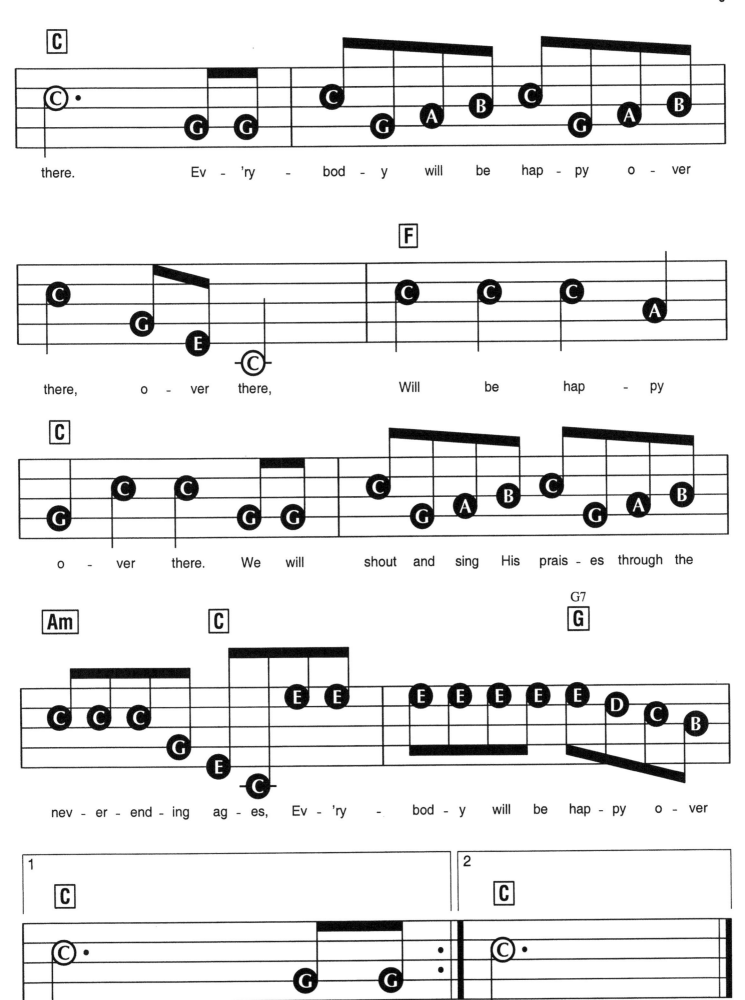

Farther Along

Registration 10
Rhythm: Waltz

Words and Music by J.R. Baxter, Jr.
and W.B. Stevens

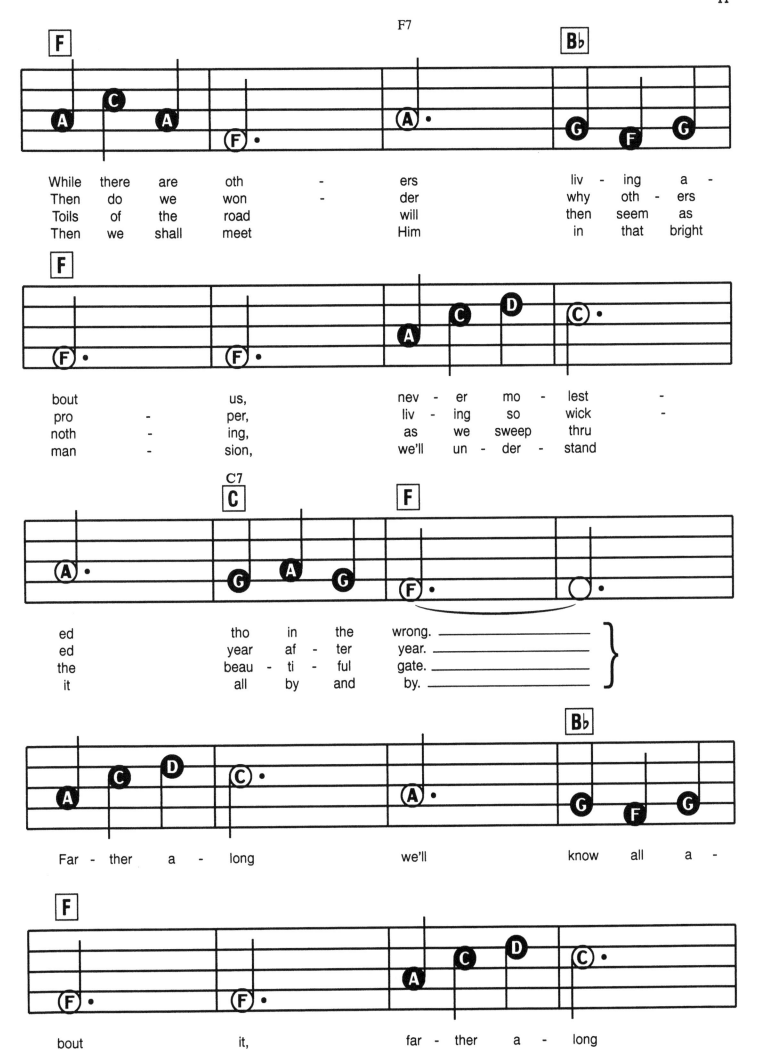

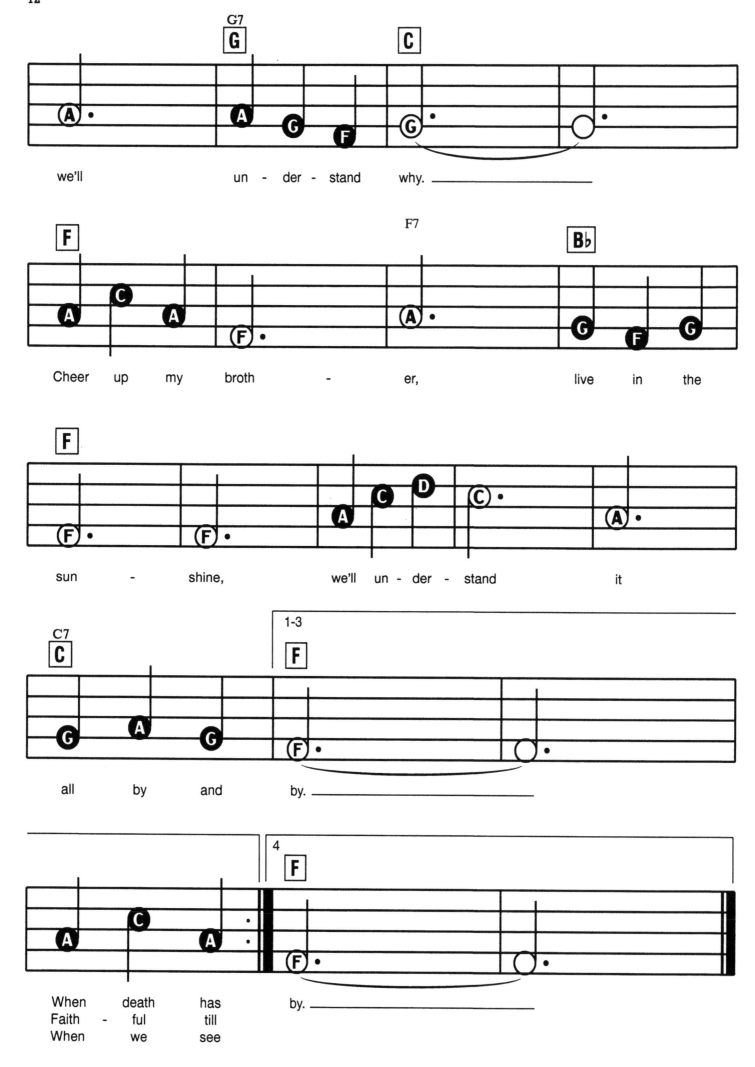

Going to Live in Green Pastures

Registration 1
Rhythm: Waltz

Words and Music by
H.W. Vanhoose

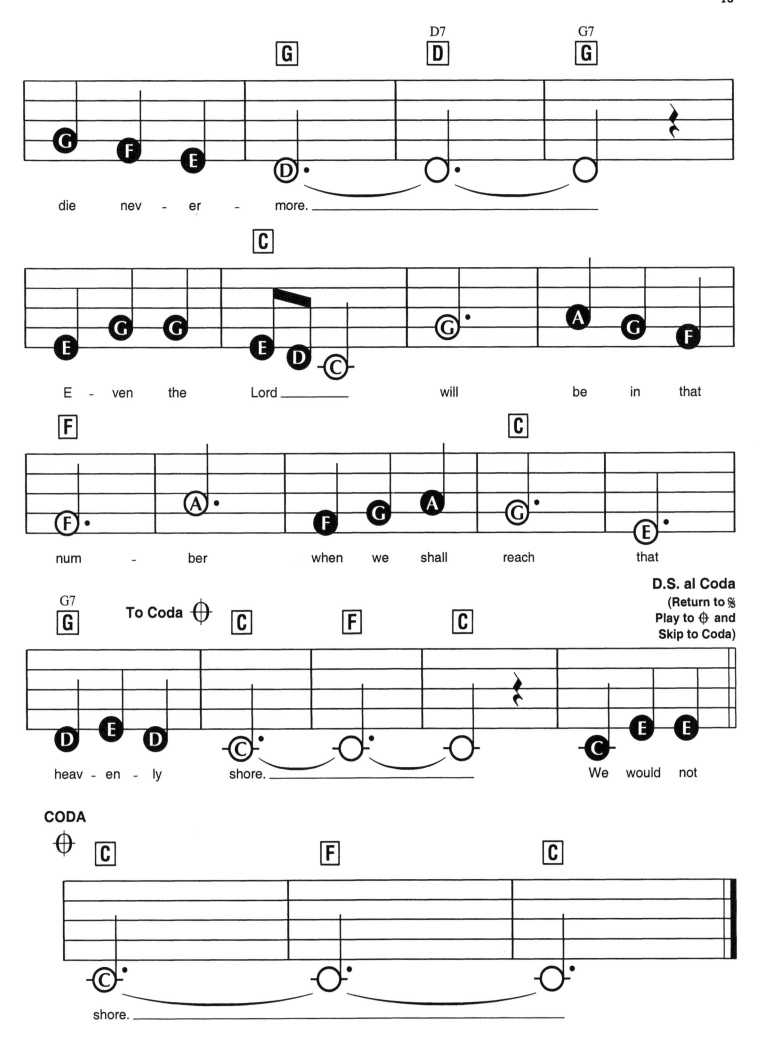

He Set Me Free

Registration 3
Rhythm: Country or Fox Trot

Words and Music by
Albert E. Brumley

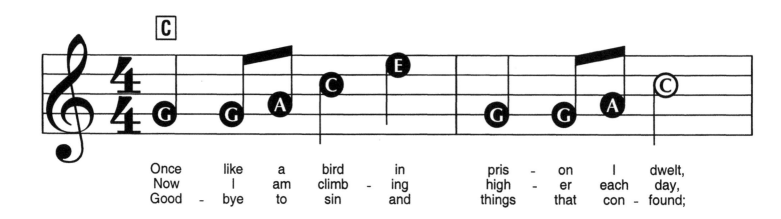

Once like a bird in pris - on I dwelt,
Now I am climb - ing high - er each day,
Good - bye to sin and things that con - found;

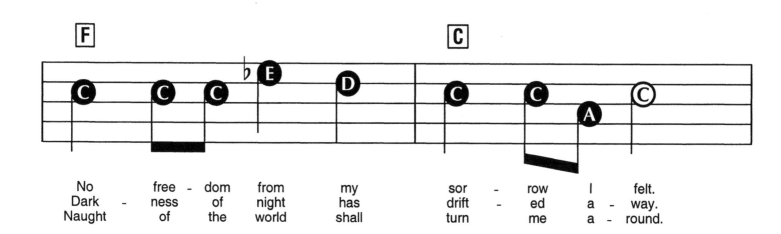

No free - dom from my sor - row I felt.
Dark - ness of night has drift - ed a - way.
Naught of the world shall turn me a - round.

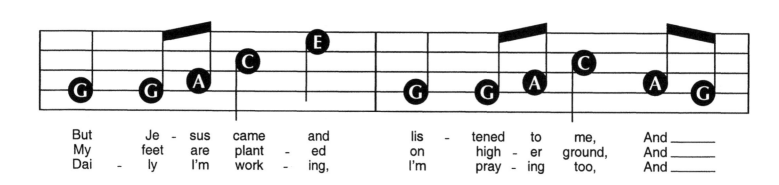

But Je - sus came and lis - tened to me, And _____
My feet are plant - ed on high - er ground, And _____
Dai - ly I'm work - ing, I'm pray - ing too, And _____

He's Got the Whole World in His Hands

Registration 6
Rhythm: Swing or Rock

Traditional Spiritual

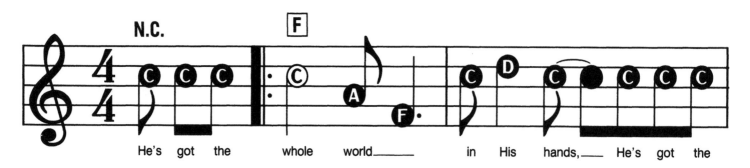

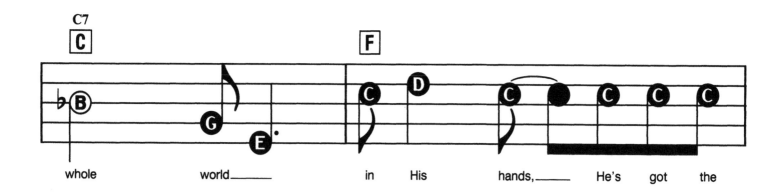

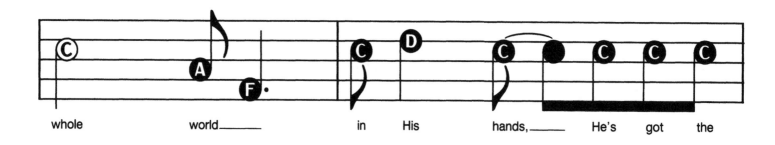

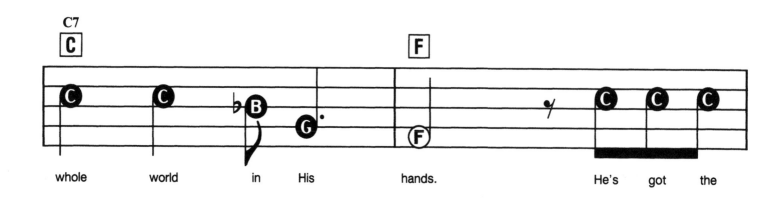

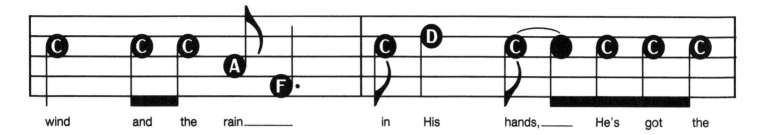

wind   and   the   rain____   in   His   hands,____   He's   got   the

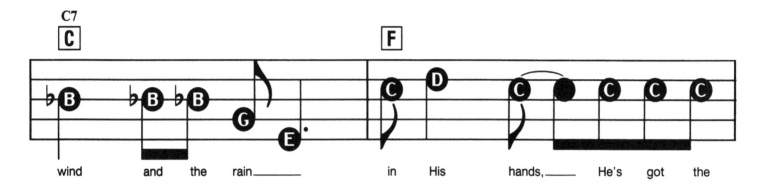

wind   and   the   rain____   in   His   hands,____   He's   got   the

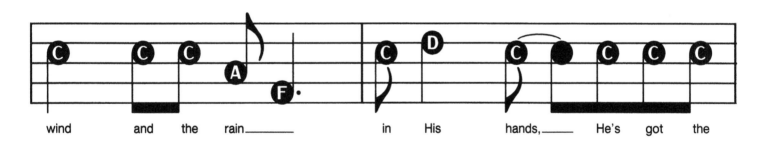

wind   and   the   rain____   in   His   hands,____   He's   got   the

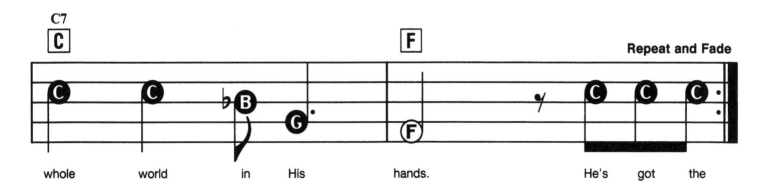

whole   world   in   His   hands.   He's   got   the

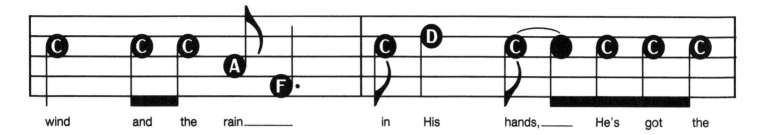19

A Home in Heaven

Registration 2
Rhythm: Waltz

Words and Music by
Hank Williams

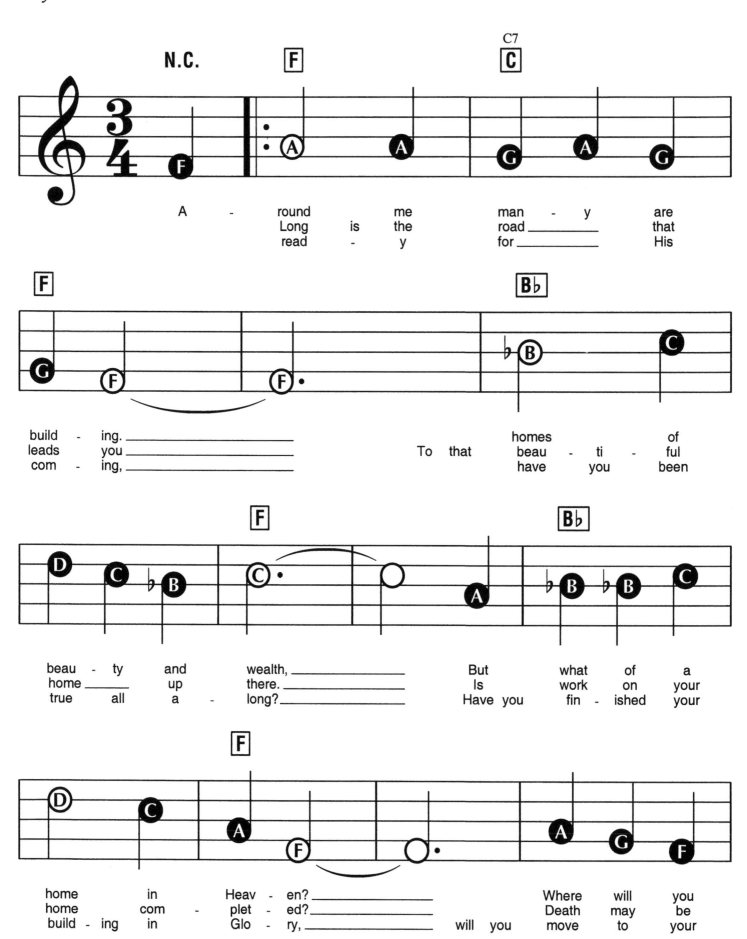

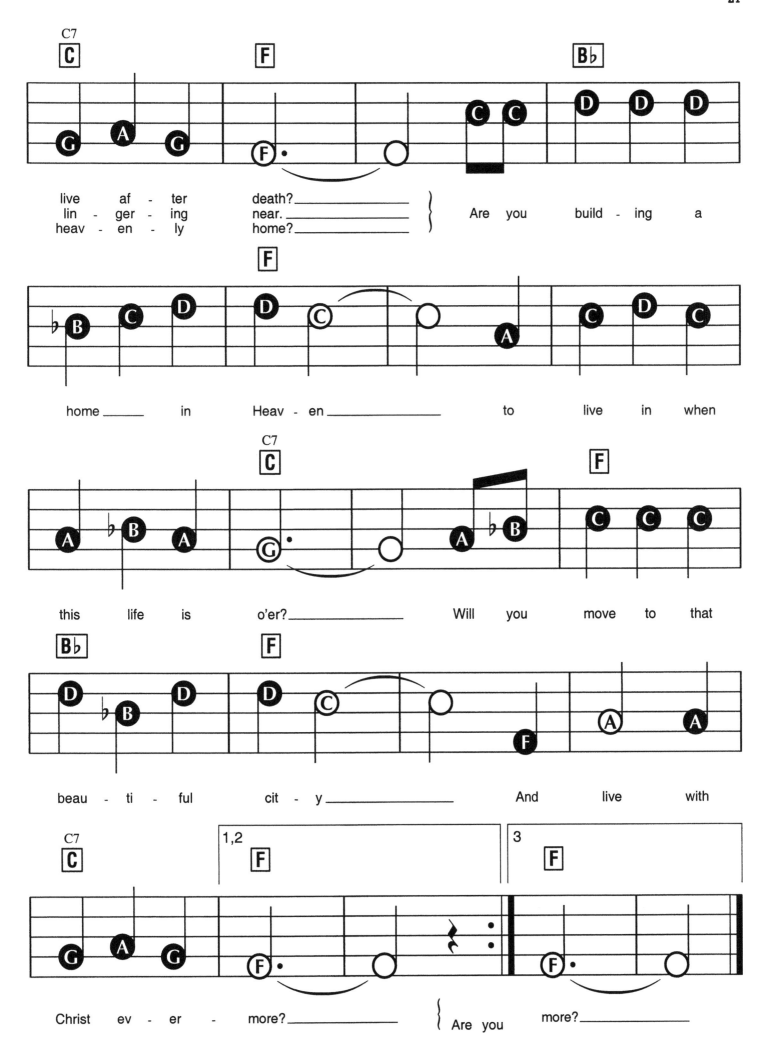

How Beautiful Heaven Must Be

Registration 1
Rhythm: Waltz

Words by Mrs. A.S. Bridgewater
Music by A.P. Bland

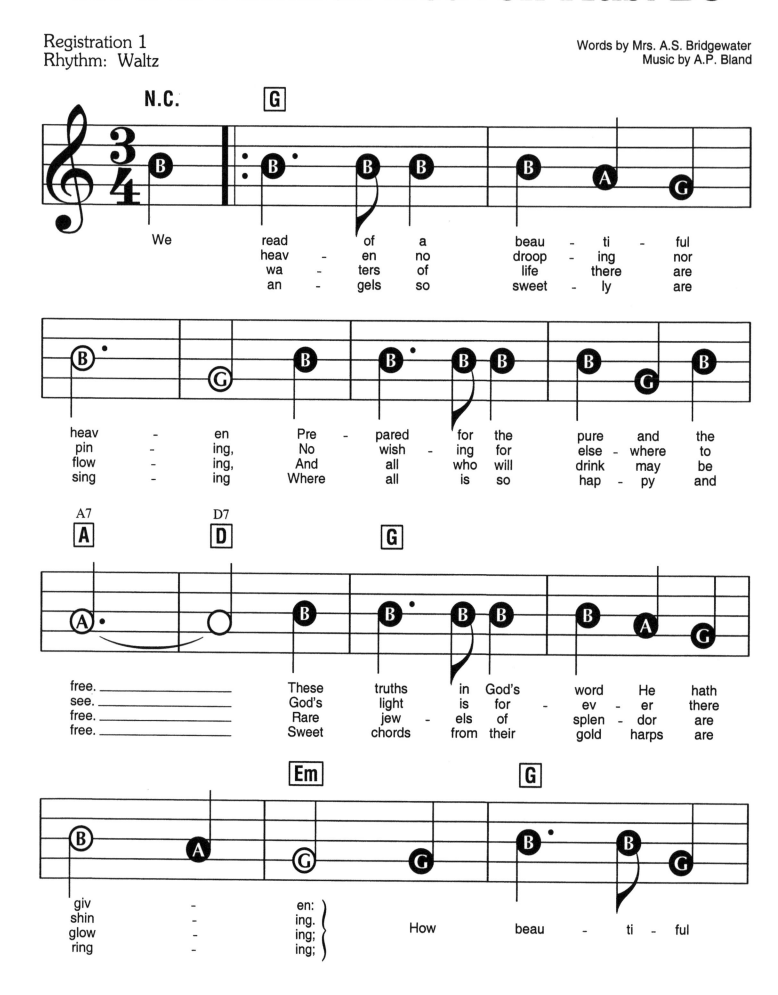

23

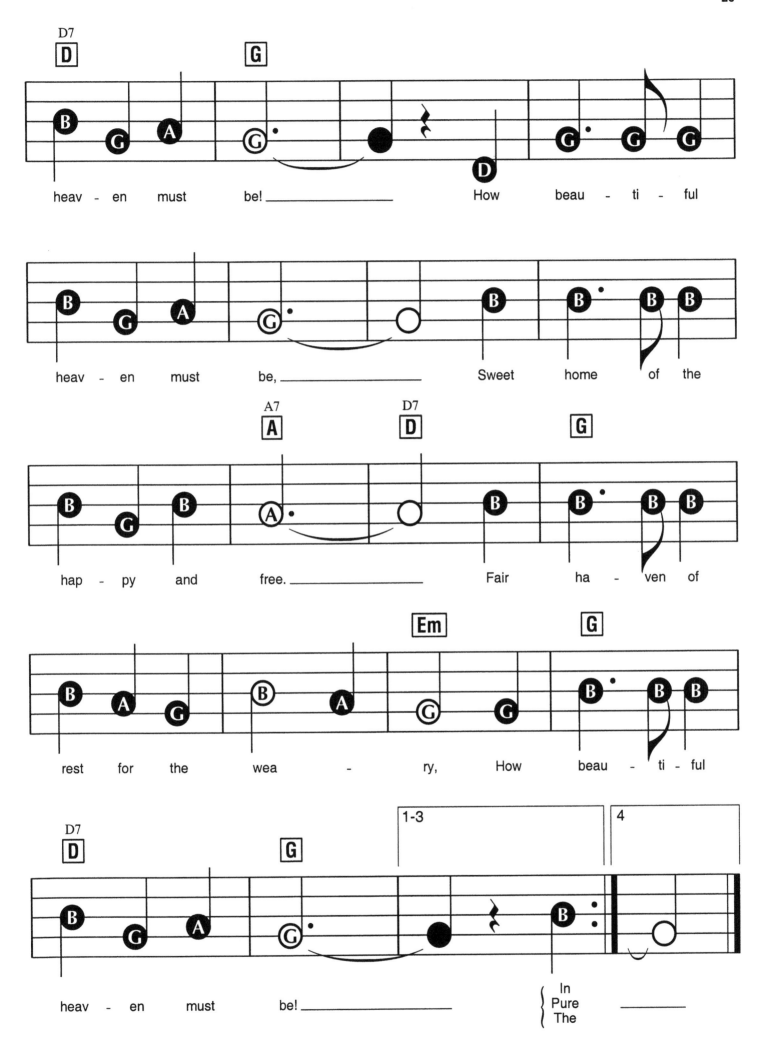

I Bowed on My Knees and Cried Holy

Registration 1
Rhythm: Waltz

Words by Nettie Dudley Washington
Music by E.M. Dudley Cantwell

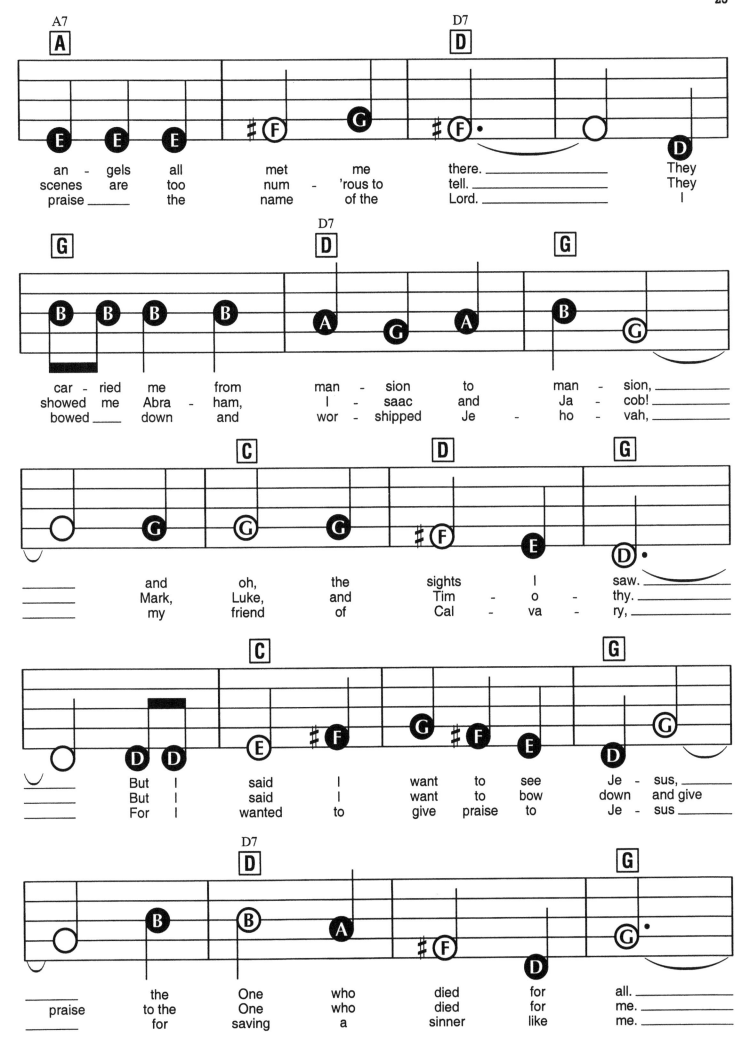

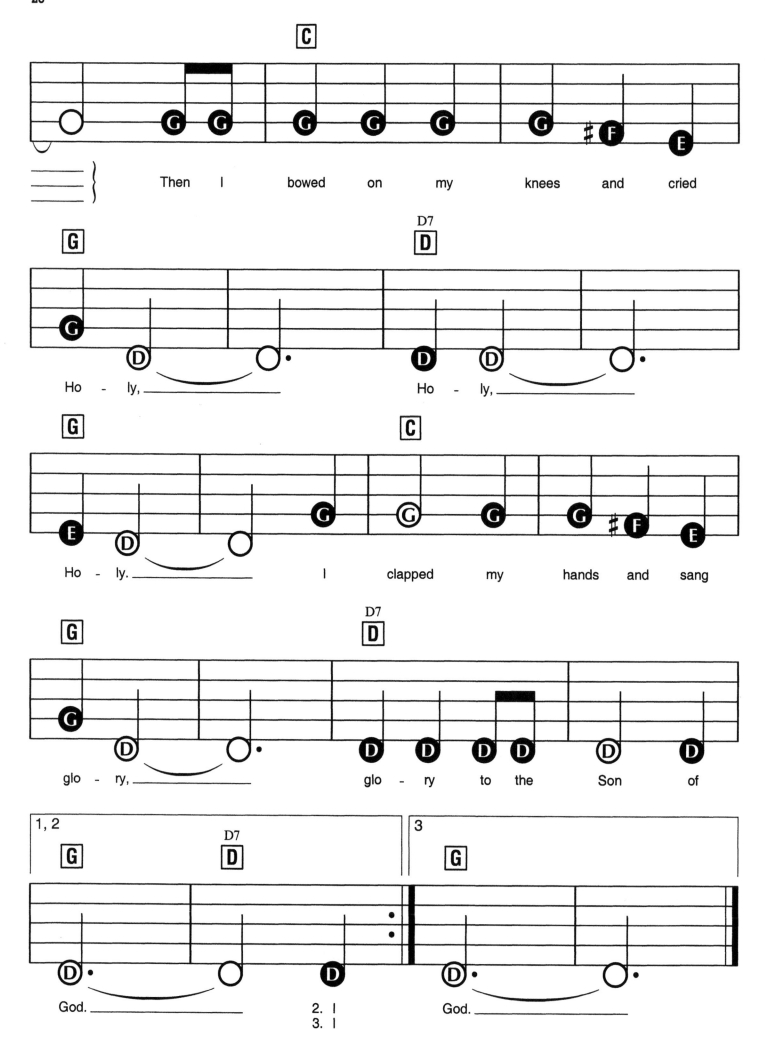

I Know Who Holds Tomorrow

Registration 1
Rhythm: Country or Ballad

Words and Music by
Ira F. Stanphill

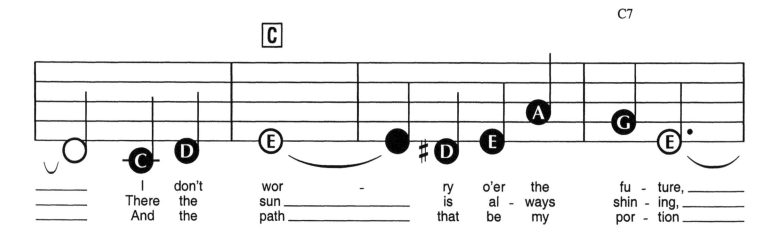

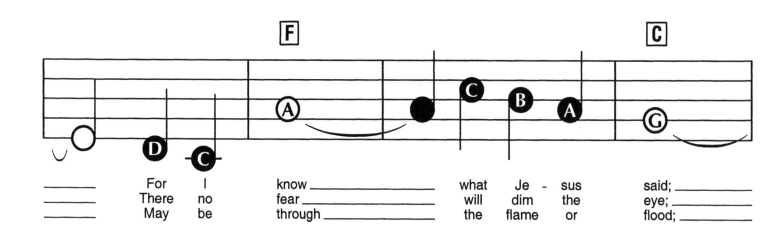

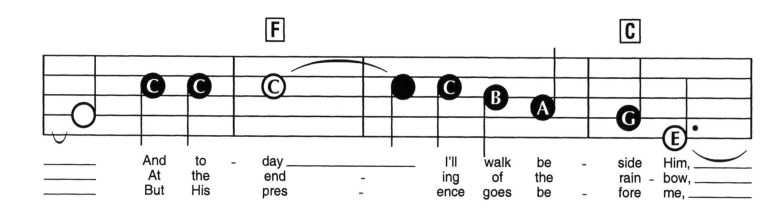

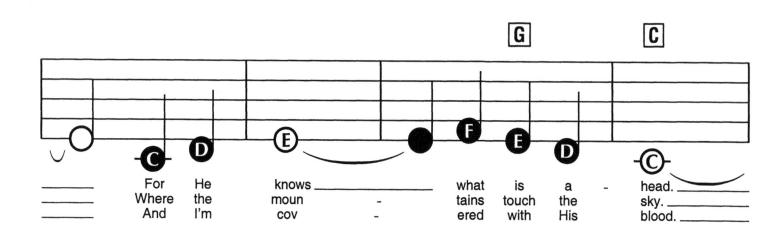

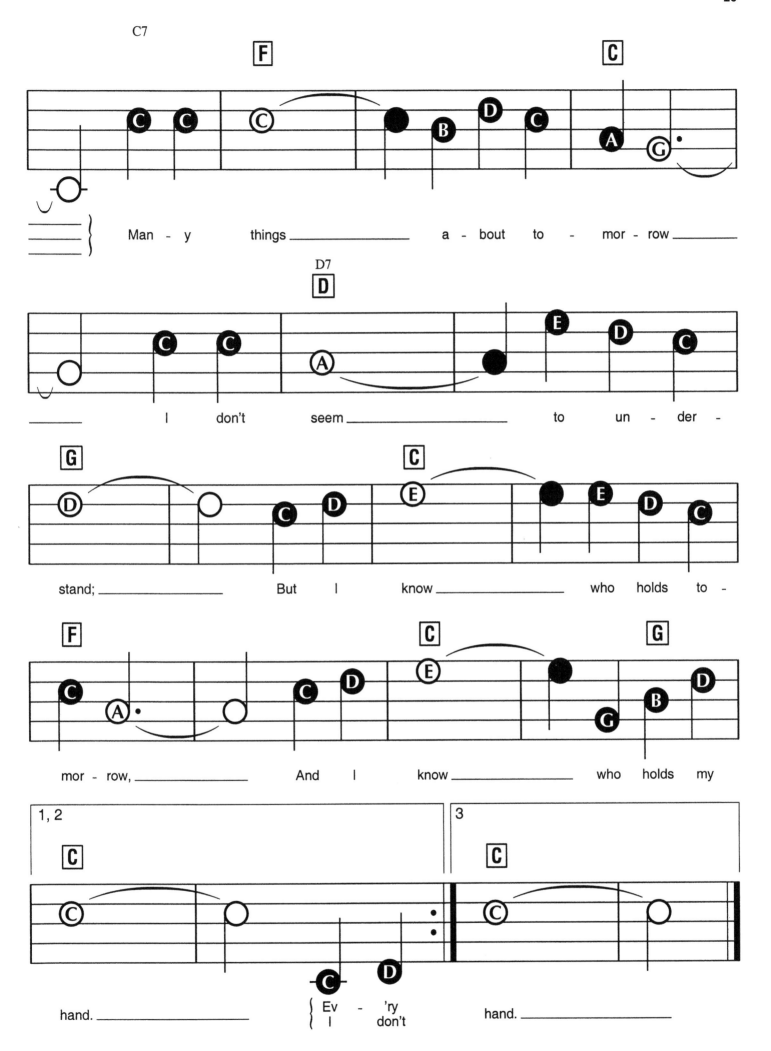

I Feel Like Traveling On

Registration 4
Rhythm: Fox Trot

Words by William Hunter
Traditional Melody
Music Arranged by James D. Vaughan

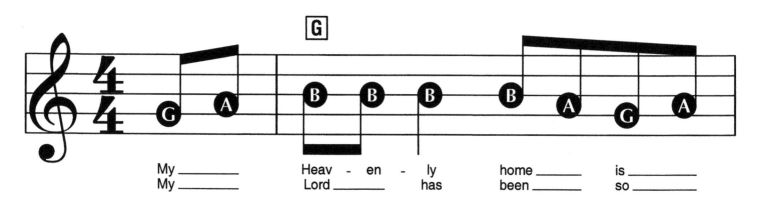

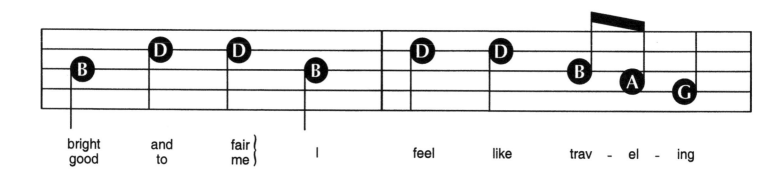

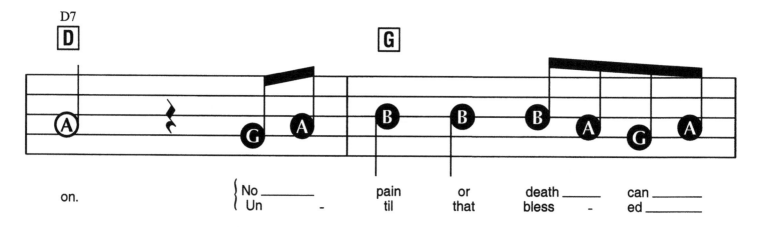

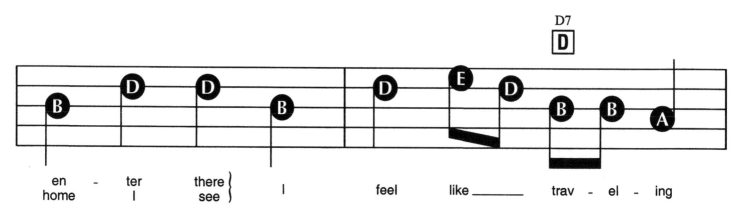

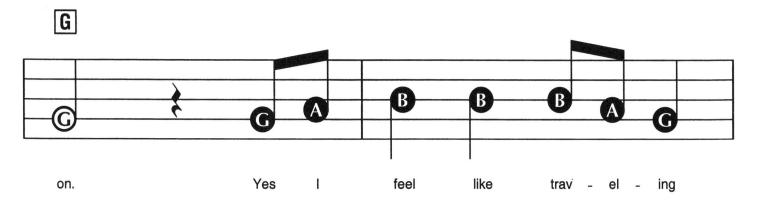

on.   Yes   I   feel   like   trav - el - ing

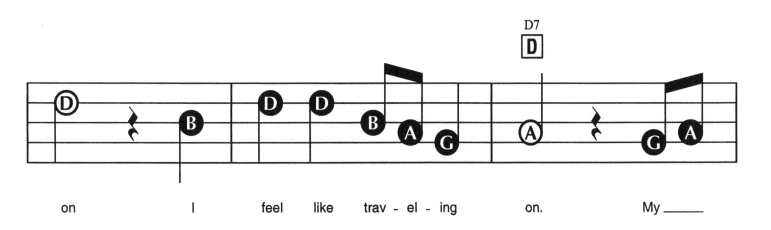

on   I   feel   like   trav - el - ing   on.   My _____

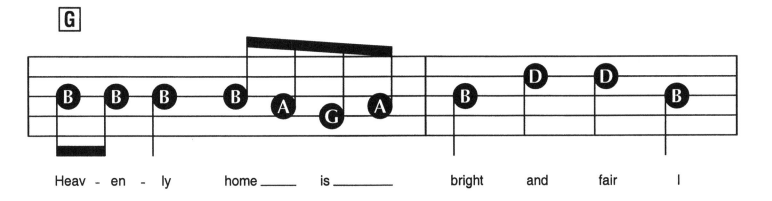

Heav - en - ly   home _____ is _____   bright   and   fair   I

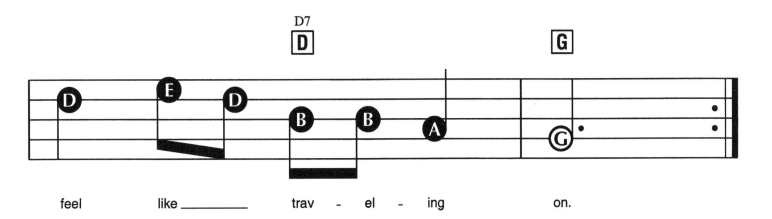

feel   like _____   trav - el - ing   on.

I Have Decided to Follow Jesus

Registration 8
Rhythm: Fox Trot

Folk Melody from India
Arranged by Auila Read

I Saw the Light

Registration 4
Rhythm: Fox Trot or Country

Words and Music by
Hank Williams

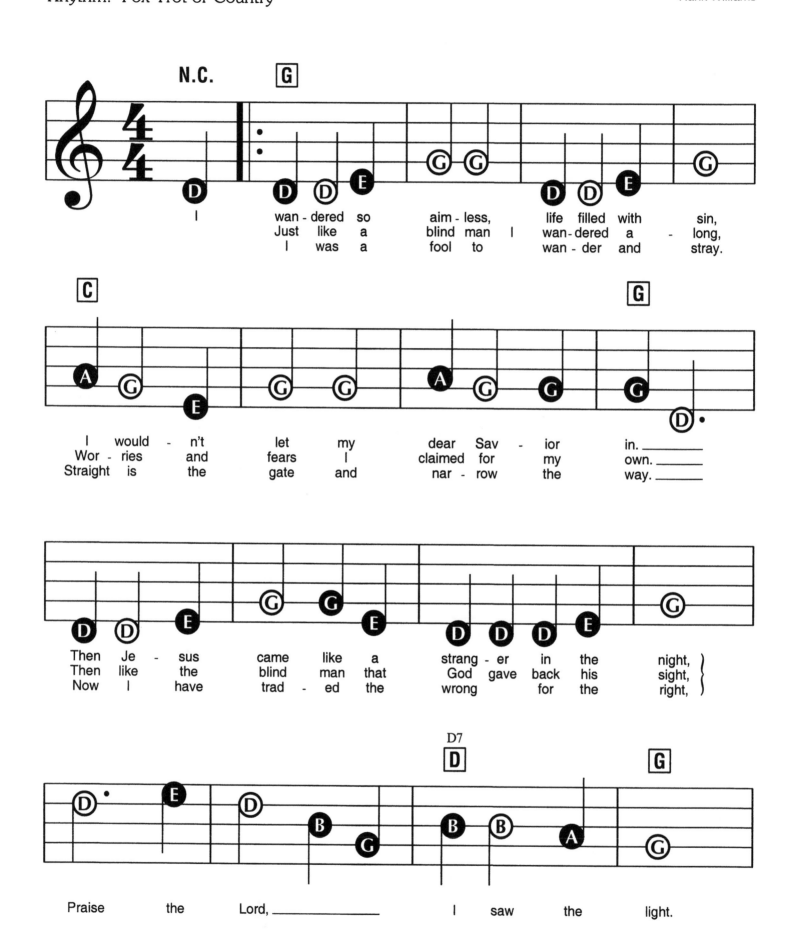

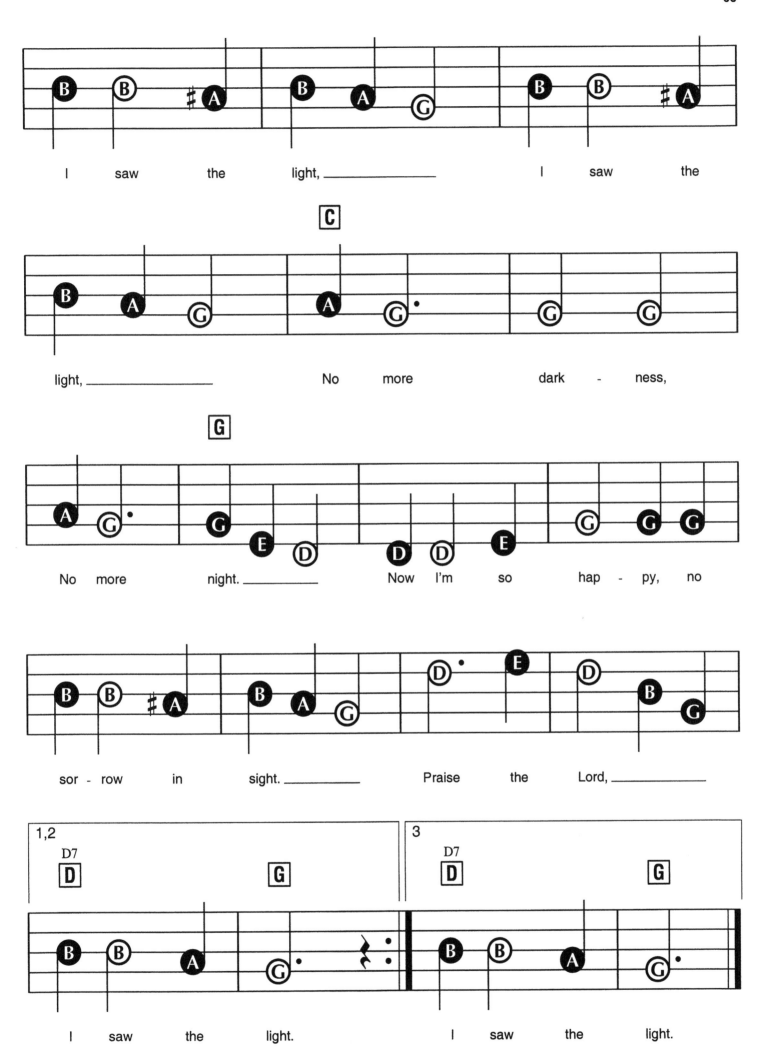

I Shall Not Be Moved

Registration 8
Rhythm: March

Words by Edward H. Boatner
American Folk Melody

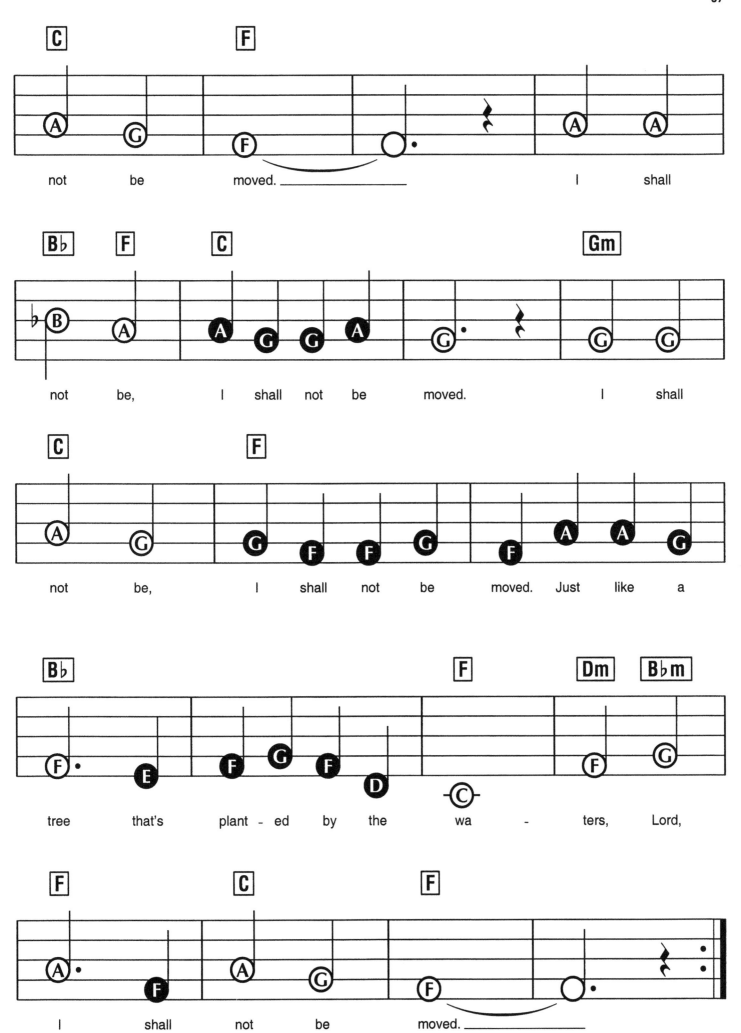

I Wouldn't Take Nothing
for My Journey Now

Registration 3
Rhythm: Fox Trot or Country

Words and Music by Jimmie Davis
and Charles F. Goodman

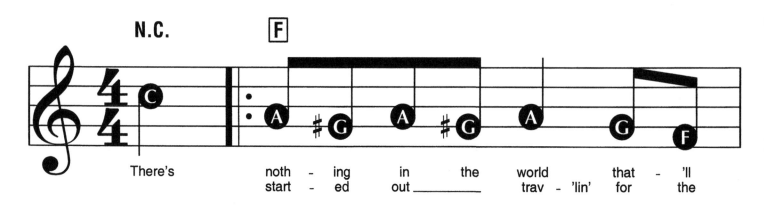

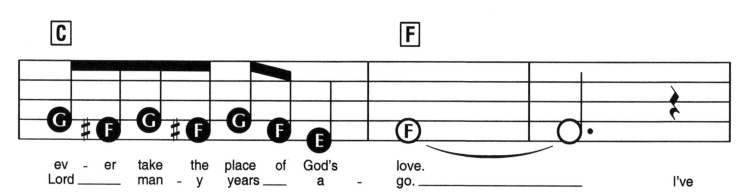

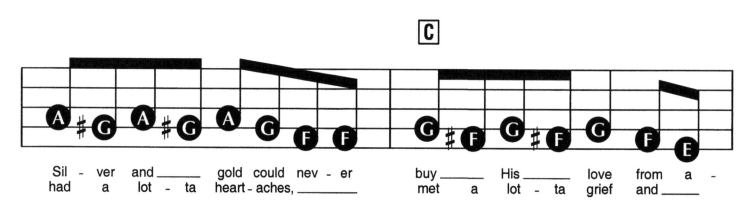

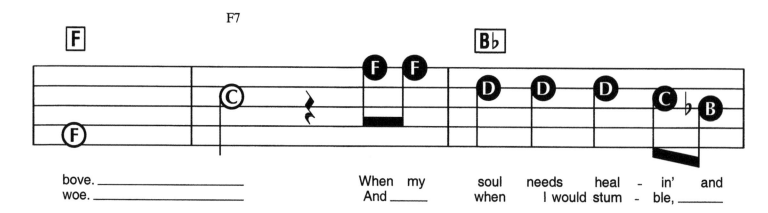

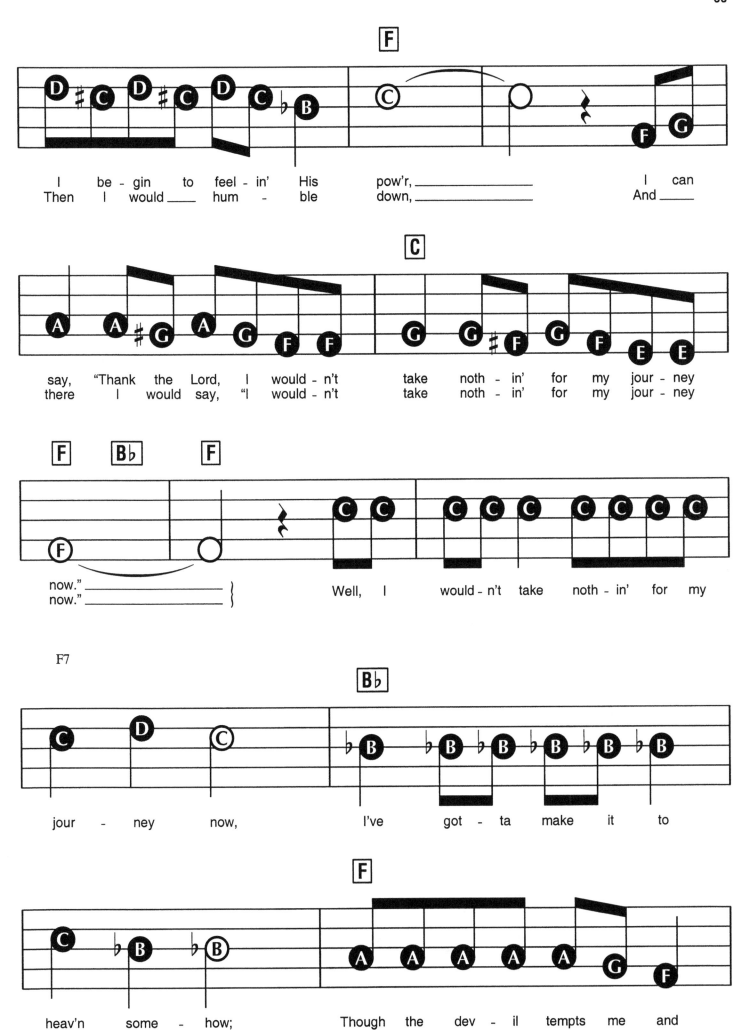

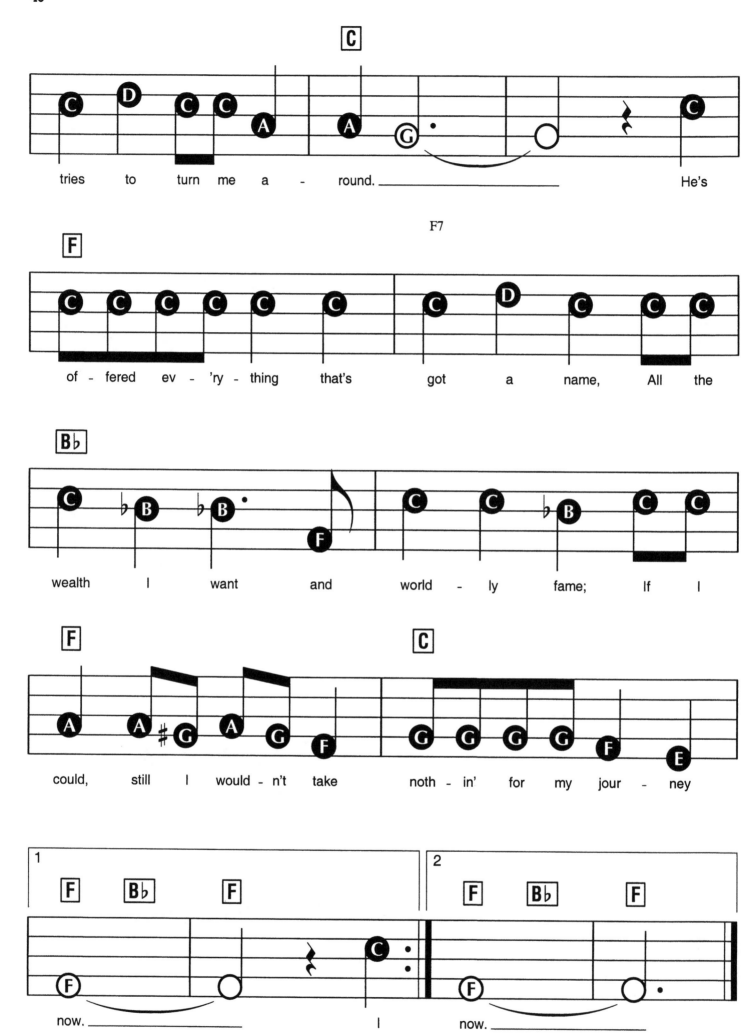

I'd Rather Be an Old Time Christian
(Than Anything I Know)

Registration 3
Rhythm: Fox Trot or Country

Words and Music by
Albert E. Brumley

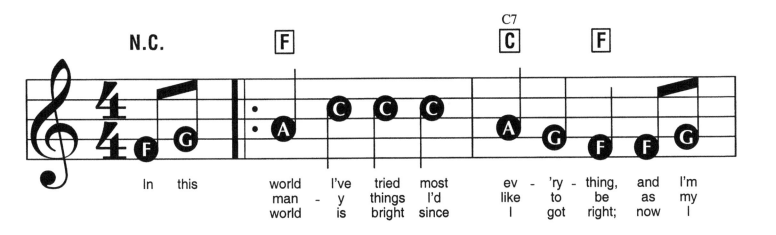

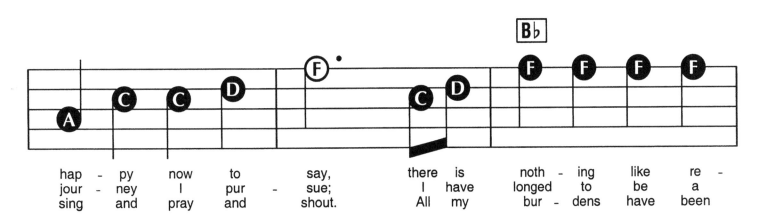

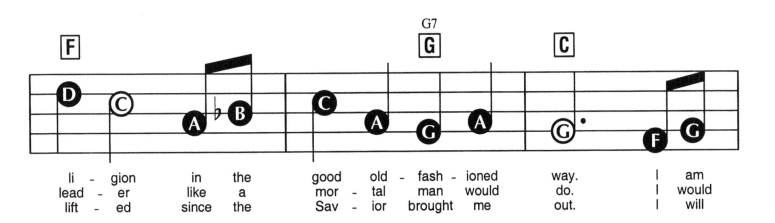

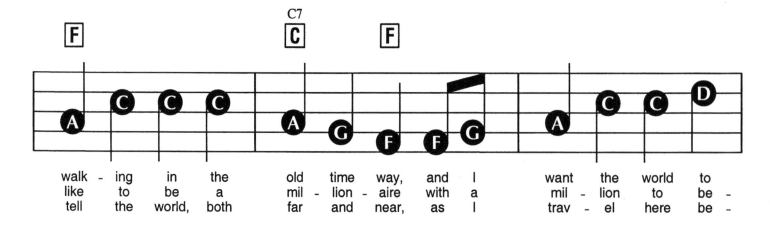

walk - ing in the old time way, and I want the world to
like to be a mil - lion - aire with a mil - lion to be -
tell the world, both far and near, as I trav - el here be -

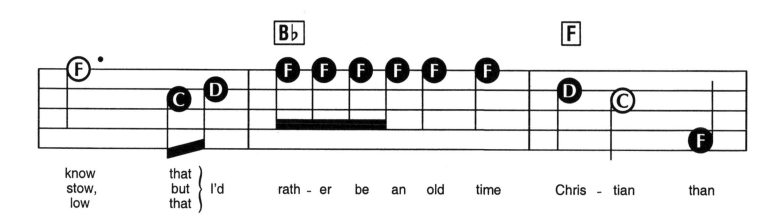

know that } I'd rath - er be an old time Chris - tian than
stow, but }
low that }

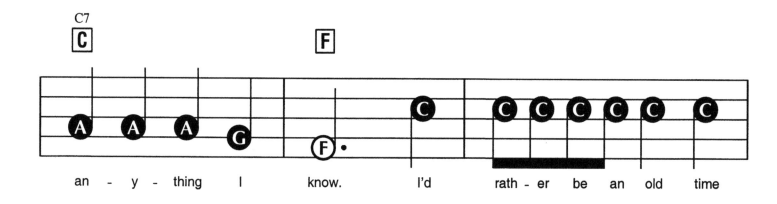

an - y - thing I know. I'd rath - er be an old time

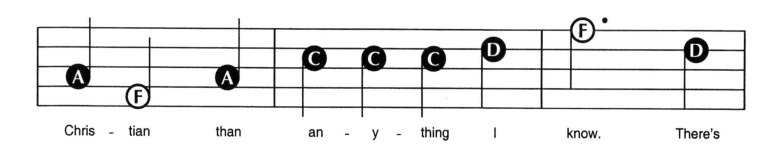

Chris - tian than an - y - thing I know. There's

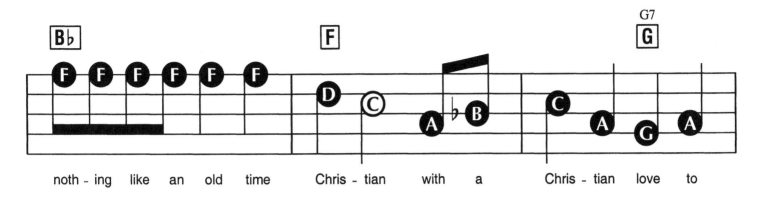

noth - ing   like   an   old   time   Chris - tian   with   a   Chris - tian   love   to

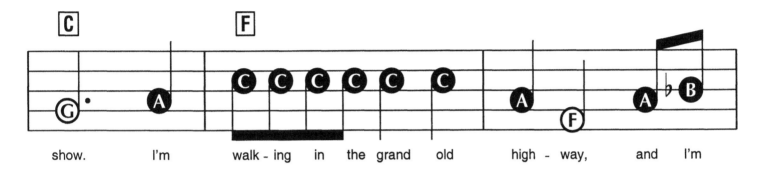

show.   I'm   walk - ing   in   the   grand   old   high - way,   and   I'm

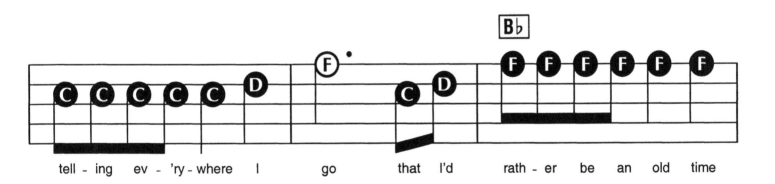

tell - ing   ev - 'ry - where   I   go   that   I'd   rath - er   be   an   old   time

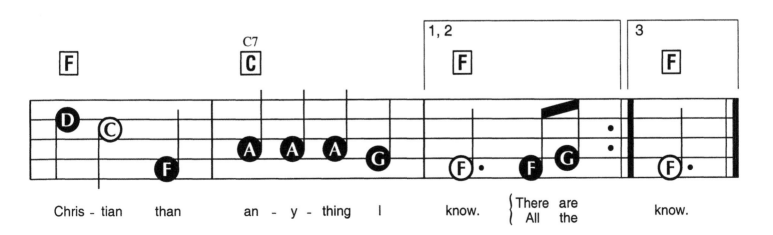

Chris - tian   than   an - y - thing   I   know.   { There are / All the }   know.

I'll Meet You in the Morning

Registration 1
Rhythm: Waltz

Words and Music by
Albert E. Brumley

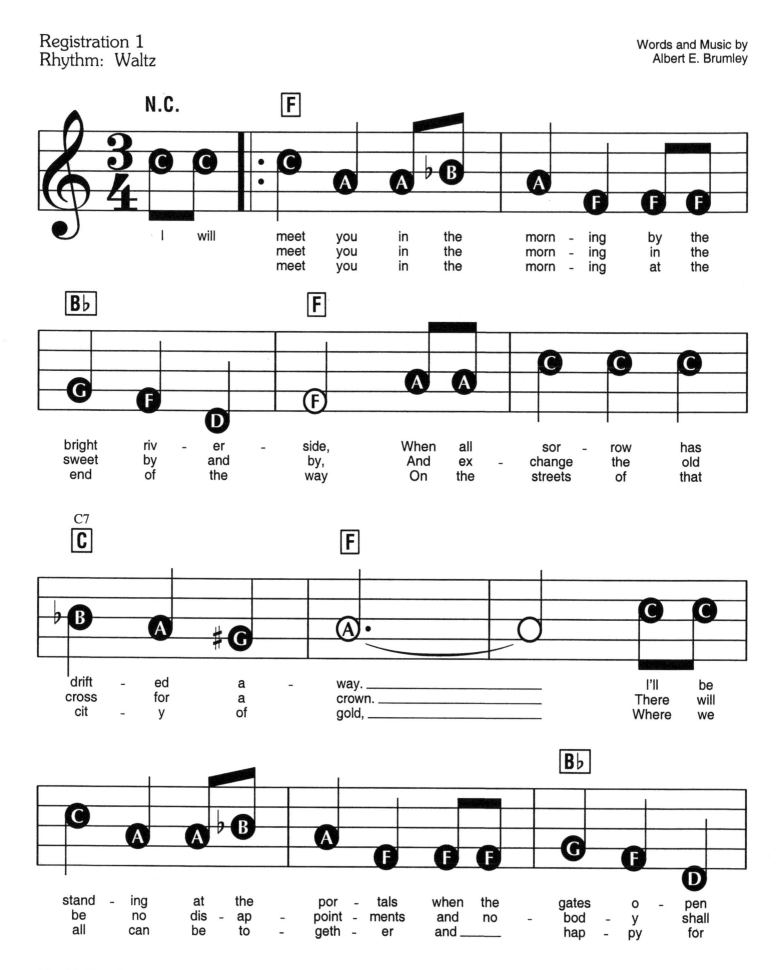

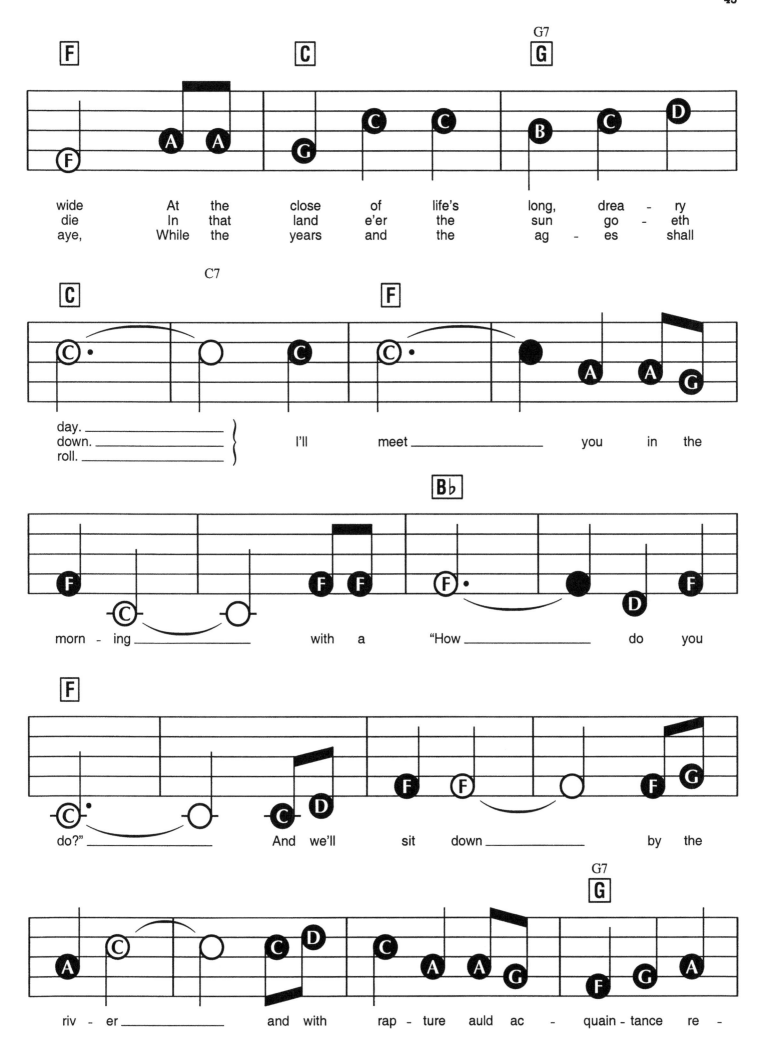

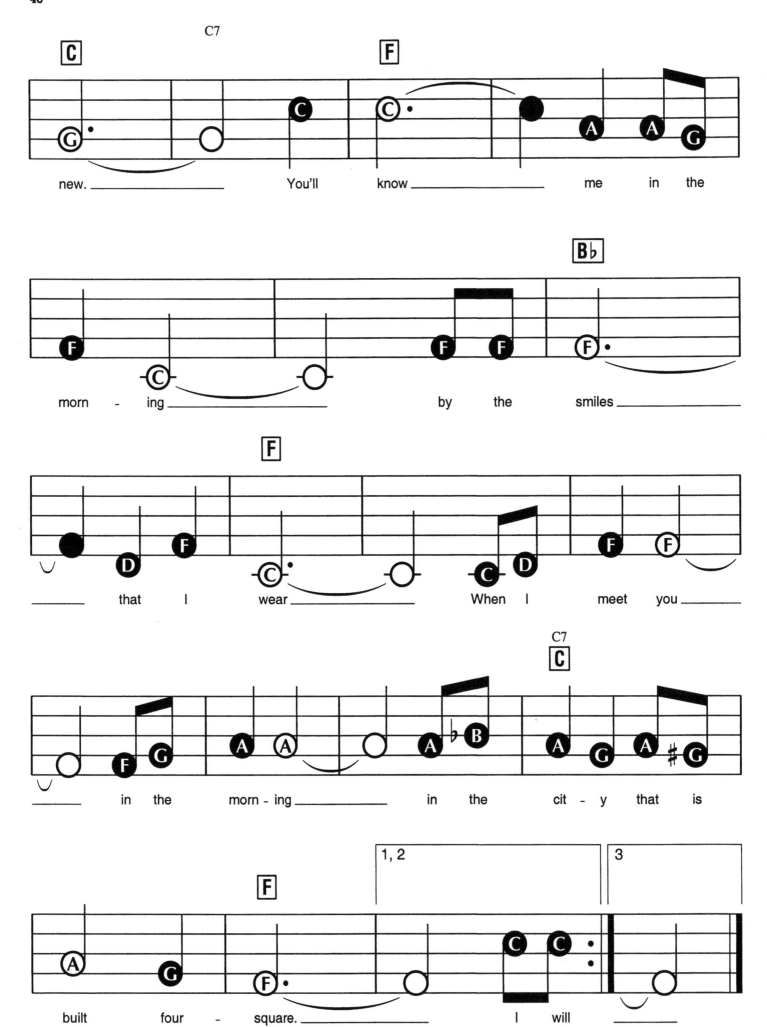

It's an Unfriendly World

Registration 3
Rhythm: Country or Swing

Words and Music by
Albert E. Brumley

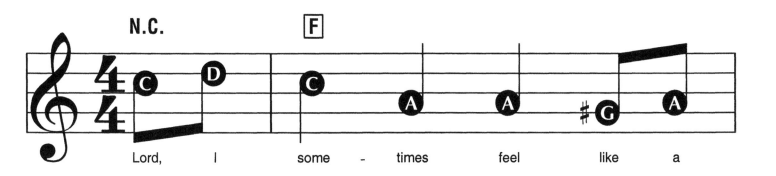

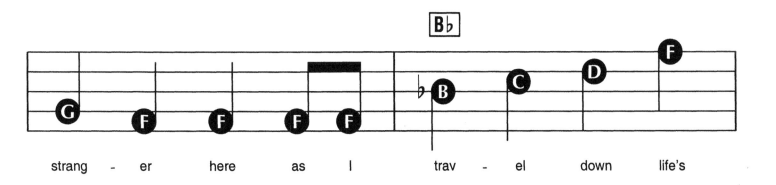

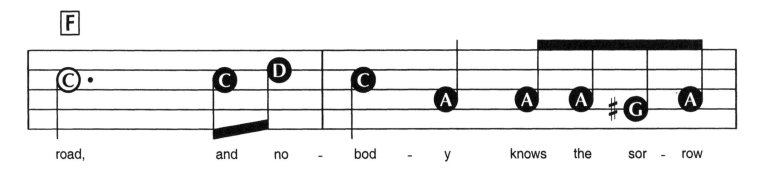

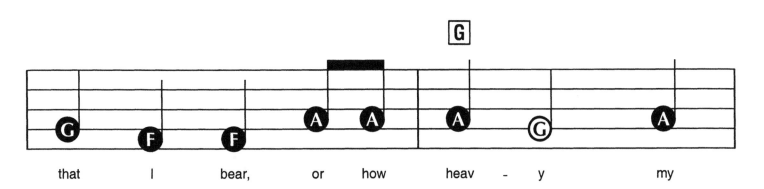

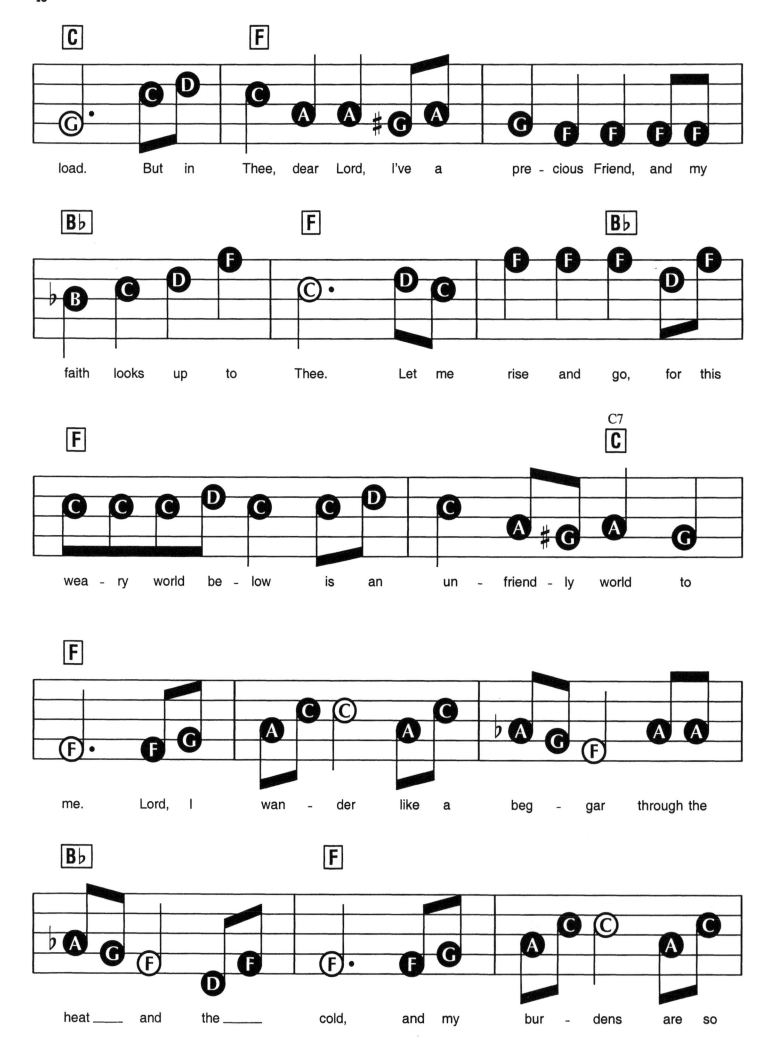

I'm On My Way to Heaven

Registration 8
Rhythm: Fox Trot

Words and Music by
Walt Mills

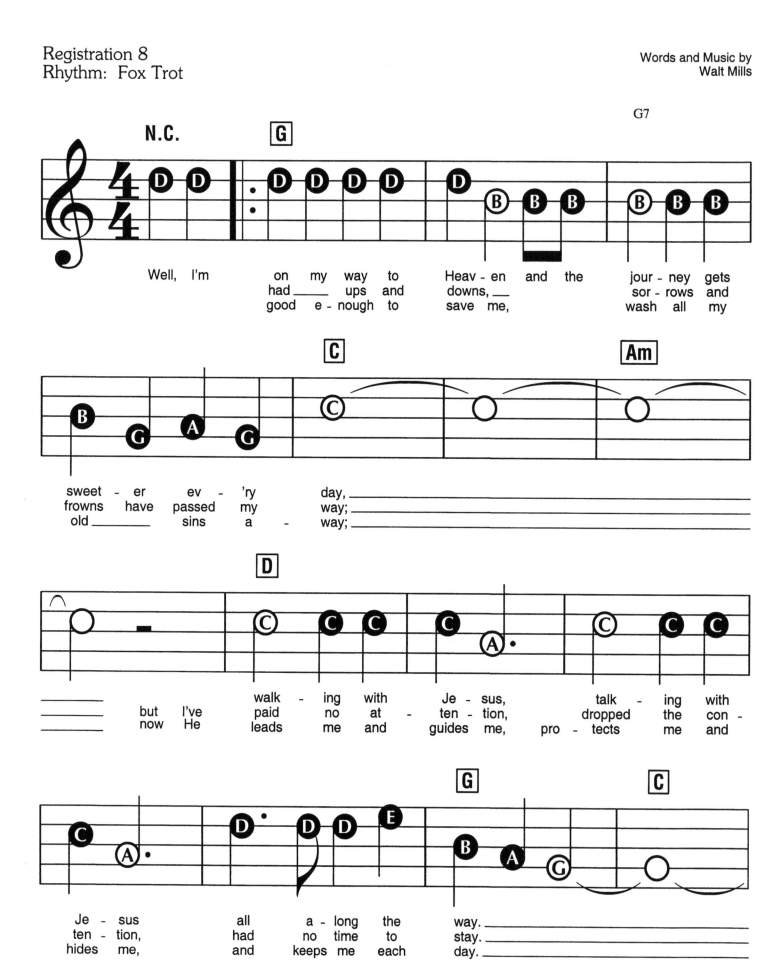

51

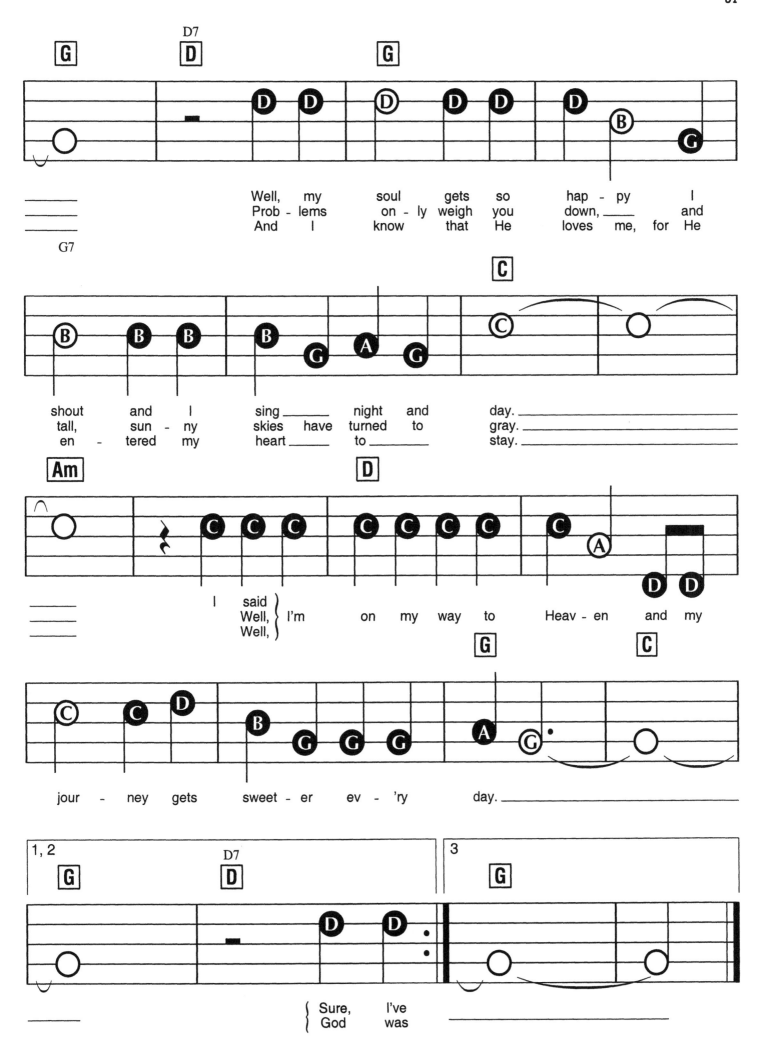

In the Garden

Words and Music by
C. Austin Miles

Registration 2
Rhythm: Waltz

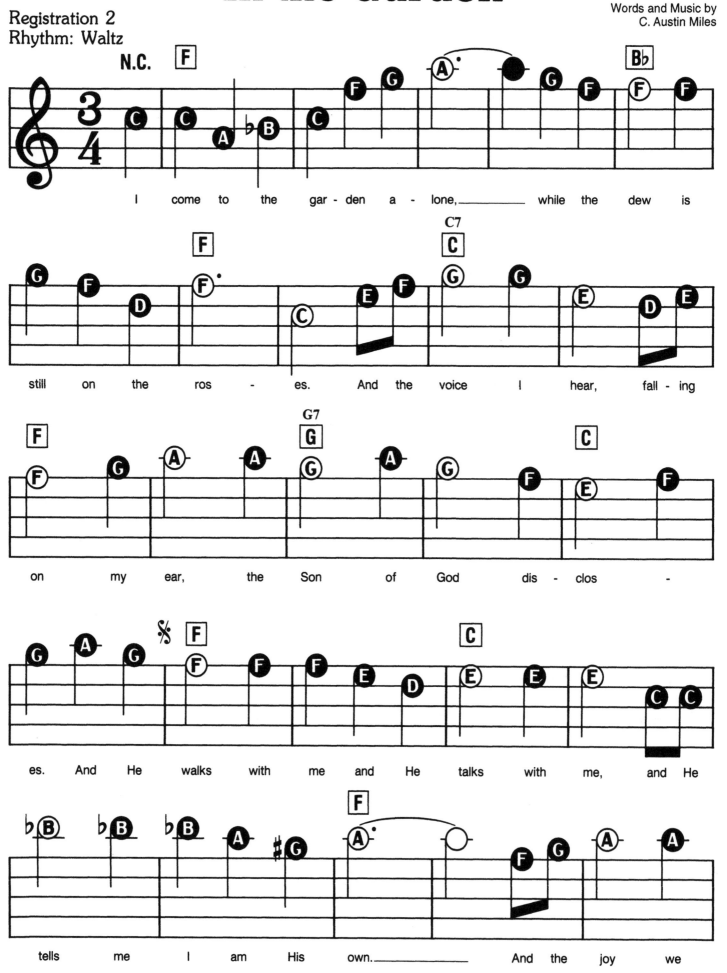

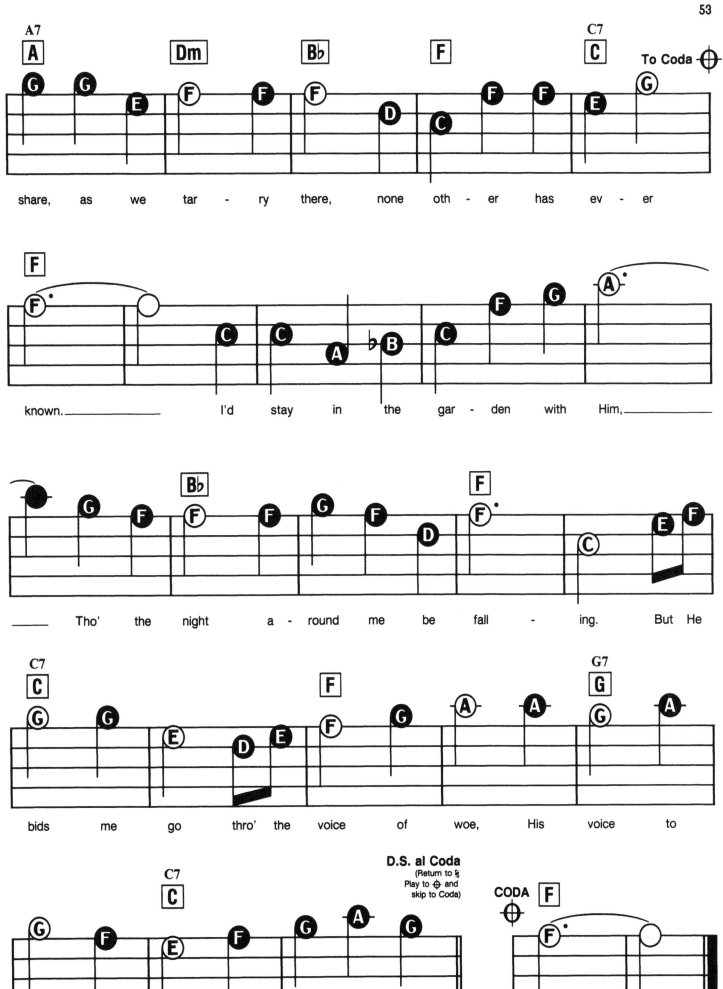

Jesus Died for Me

Registration 9
Rhythm: Country

Words and Music by
Hank Williams

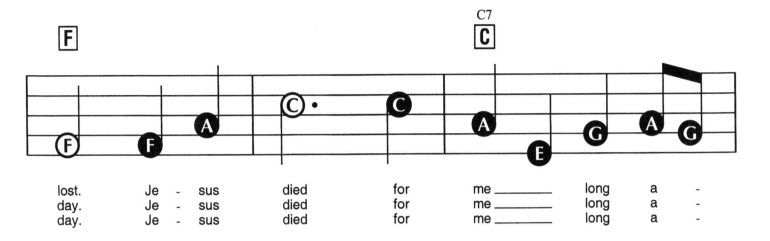

lost.   Je - sus   died   for   me _____ long   a -
day.   Je - sus   died   for   me _____ long   a -
day.   Je - sus   died   for   me _____ long   a -

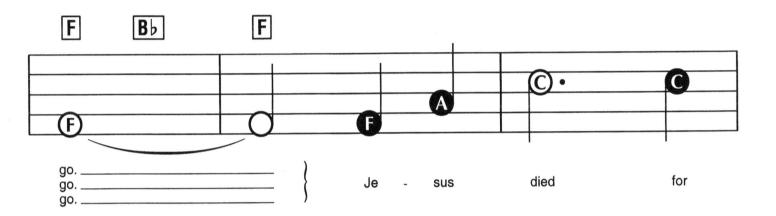

go. _____
go. _____   Je - sus   died   for
go. _____

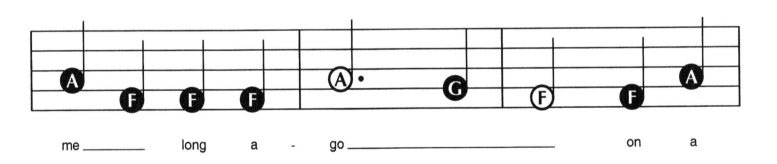

me _____ long   a - go _____ on   a

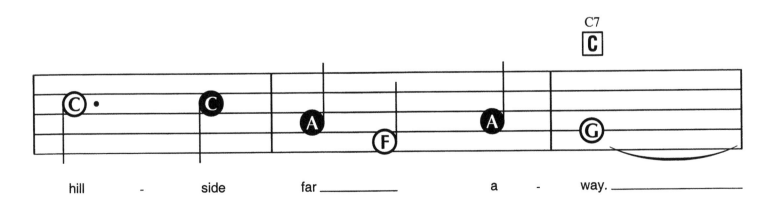

hill - side   far _____ a - way. _____

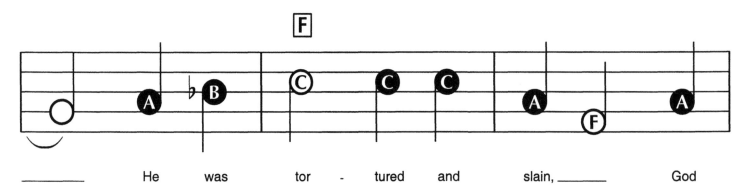

He was tor - tured and slain, _____ God

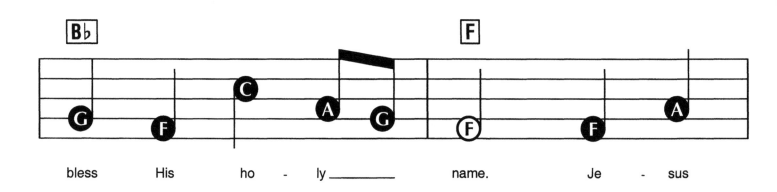

bless His ho - ly _____ name. Je - sus

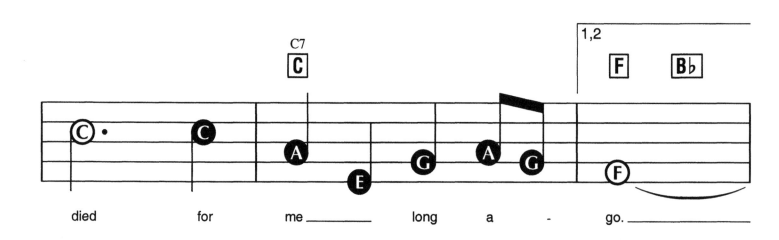

died for me _____ long a - go. _____

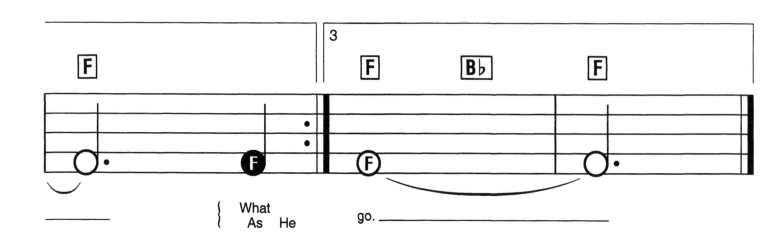

_____ { What go. _____
As He

Kum Ba Yah

Registration 3
Rhythm: Rock

Traditional Spiritual

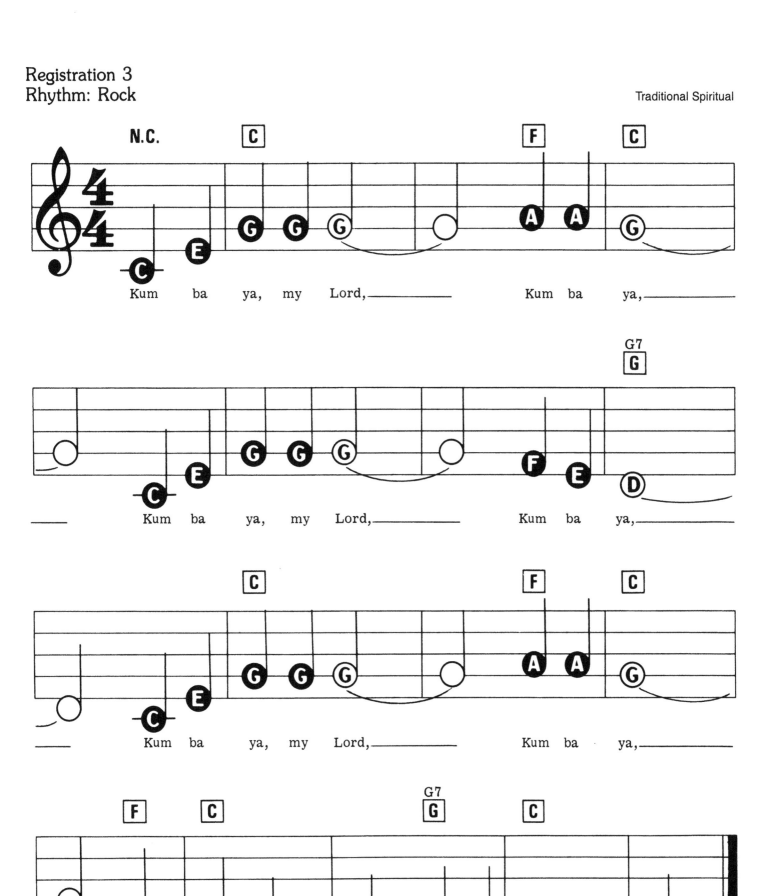

Just a Closer Walk with Thee

Registration 2
Rhythm: Swing

Traditional
Arranged by Kenneth Morris

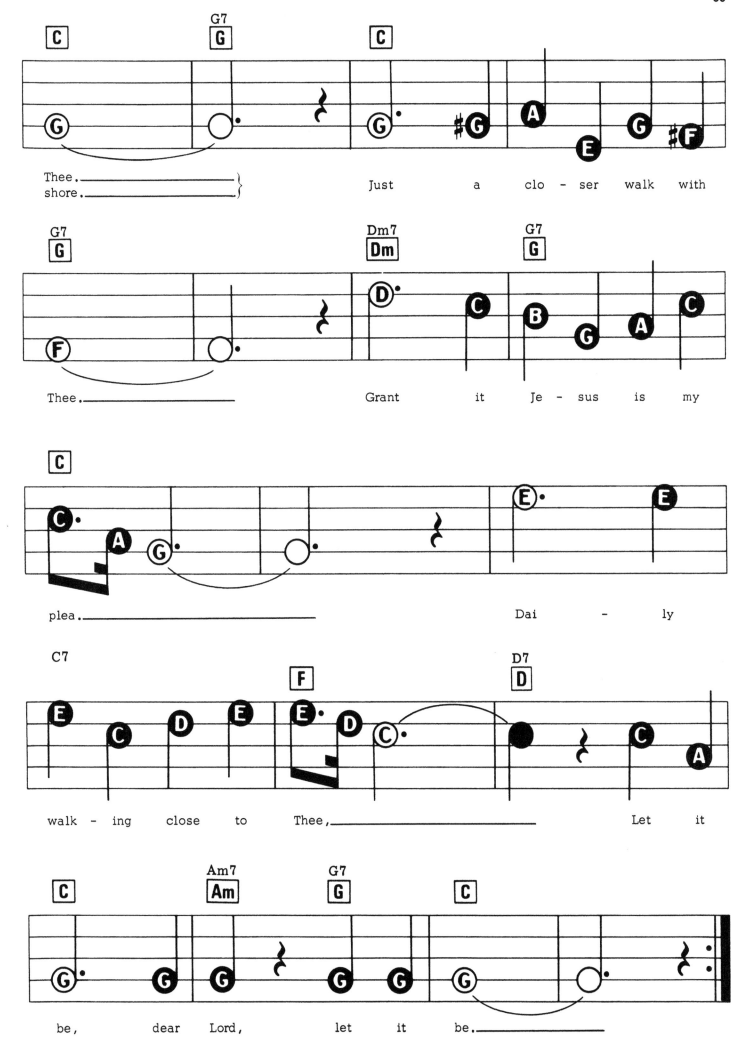

Just a Rose Will Do

Registration 4
Rhythm: Waltz

Words and Music by
J.A. McClung

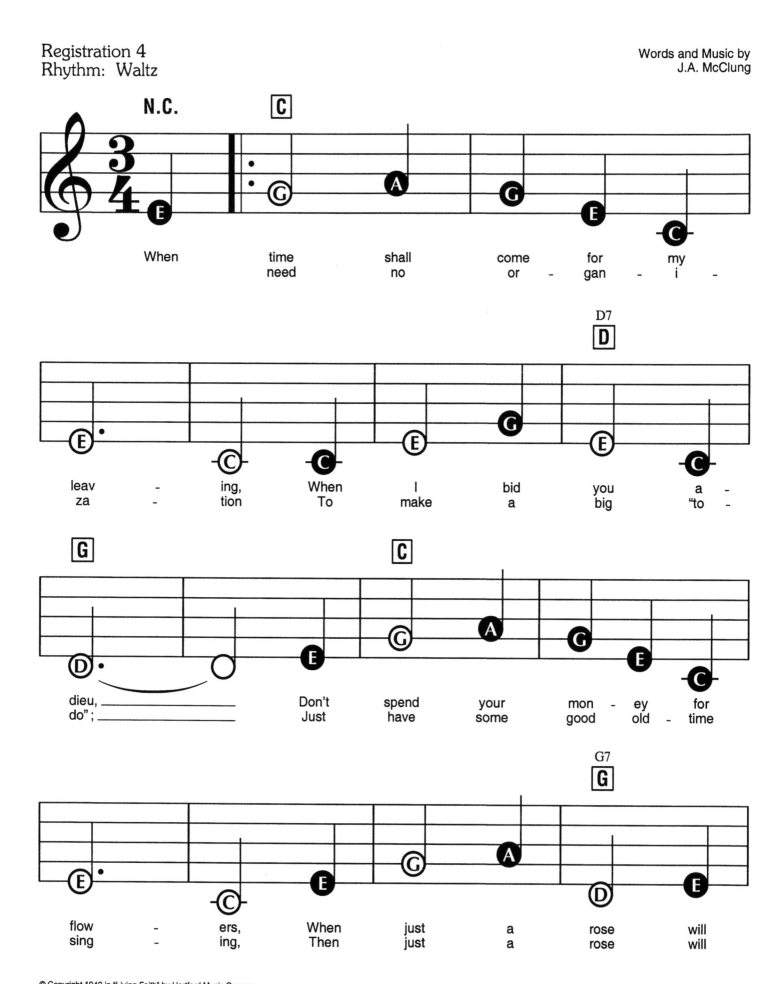

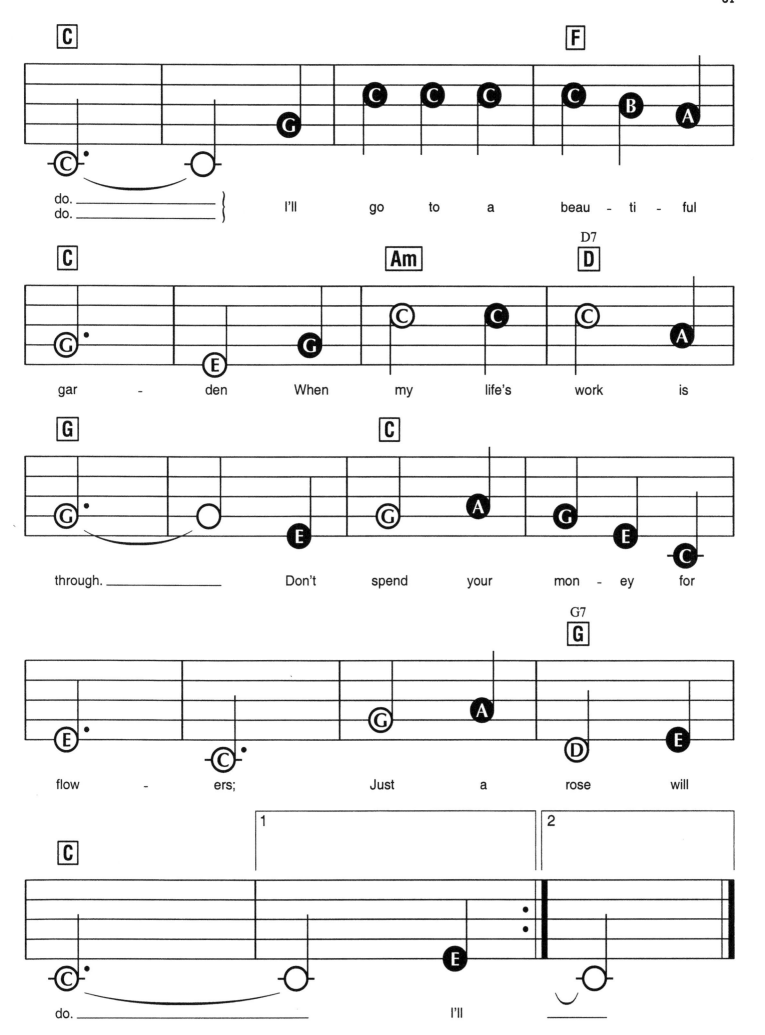

Keep On the Firing Line

Registration 2
Rhythm: March or 8 Beat

Words and Music by
J.R. Baxter, Jr.

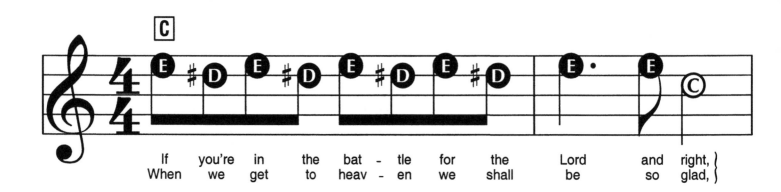

If you're in the bat - tle for the Lord and right,
When we get to heav - en we shall be so glad,

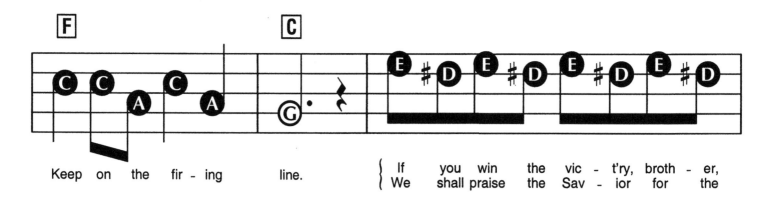

Keep on the fir - ing line.
{ If you win the vic - t'ry, broth - er,
{ We shall praise the Sav - ior for the

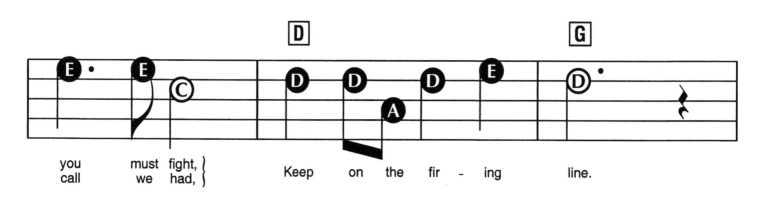

you must fight,
call we had,
Keep on the fir - ing line.

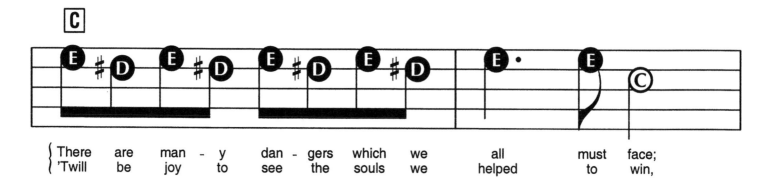

{ There are man - y dan - gers which we all must face;
{ 'Twill be joy to see the souls we helped to win,

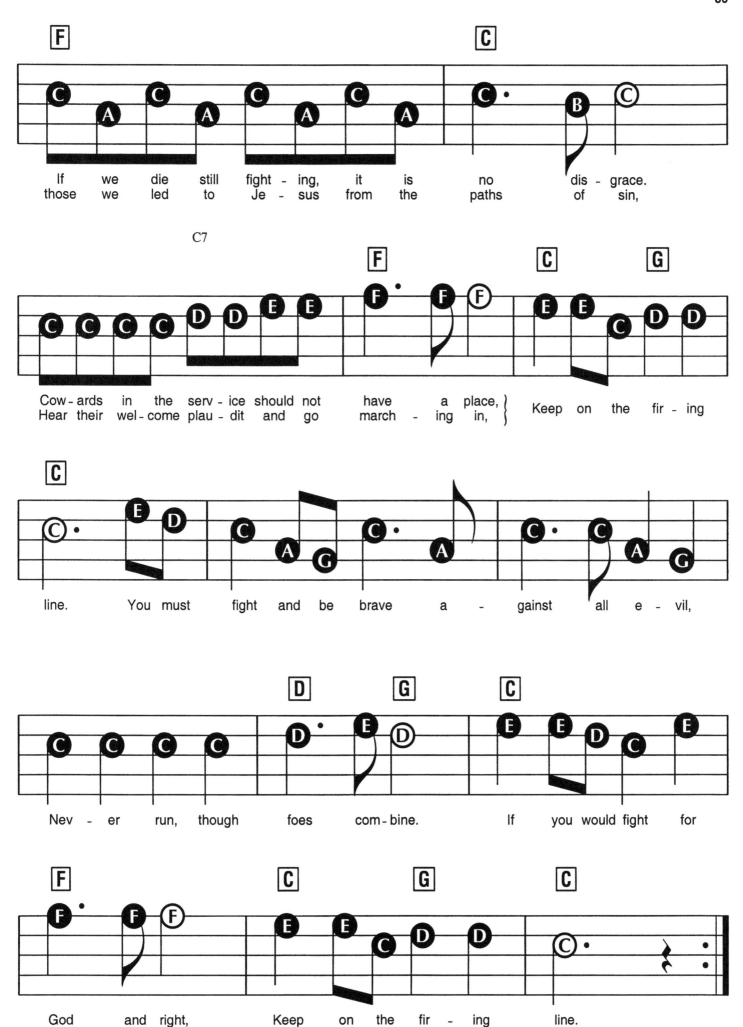

Light at the End of the Darkness

Registration 1
Rhythm: Country or Ballad

Words and Music by
Larry Gatlin

There's a / light at the / end of the
hope in that / light for the

dark — ness, And it shines _____ for
hope — less, And a sooth - ing balm for

all the world to see. It will
pain and mis - er - y. It's as

shine on your heart if you will let
near as your faith, but some - times seems let

fleet —

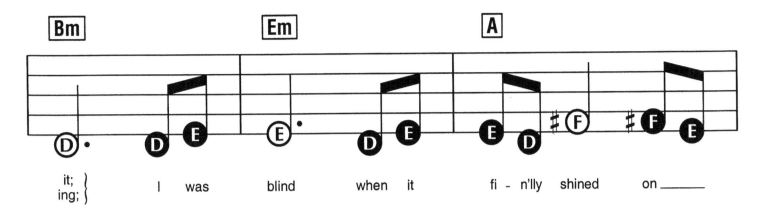

it; / ing;   I was blind when it fi - n'lly shined on _____

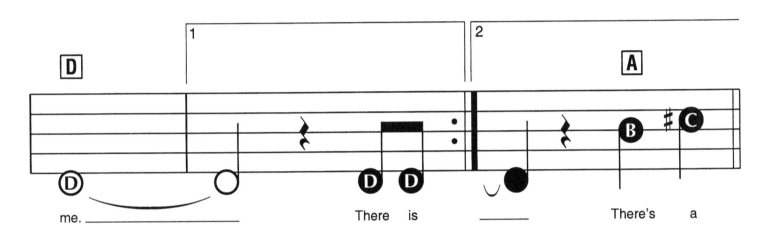

me. _____   There is _____ There's a

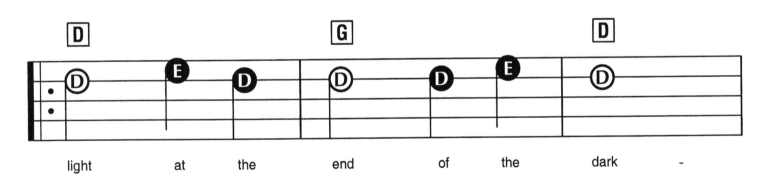

light at the end of the dark -

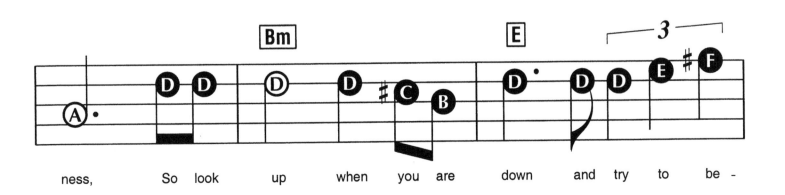

ness, So look up when you are down and try to be -

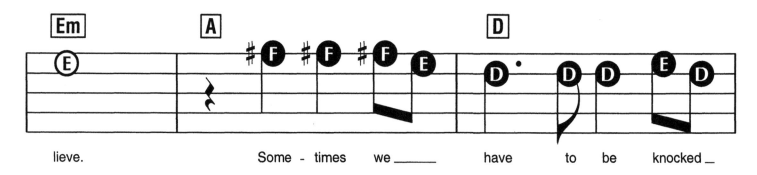

lieve.   Some - times   we _____   have   to   be   knocked _

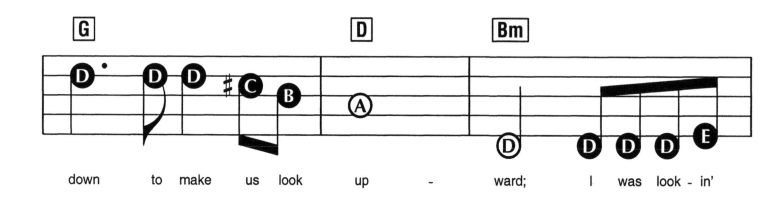

down   to   make   us   look   up   -   ward;   I   was   look - in'

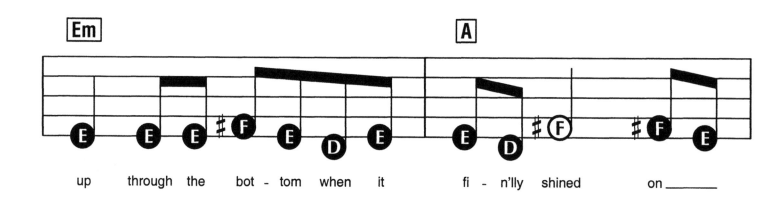

up   through   the   bot - tom   when   it   fi - n'lly   shined   on _____

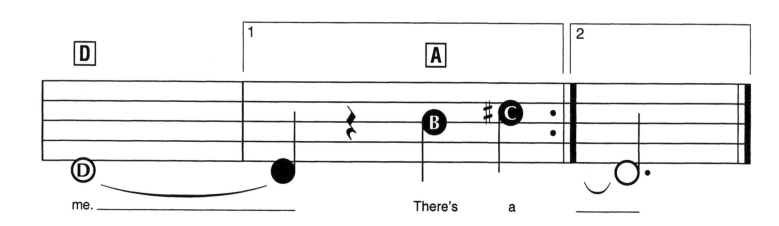

me. _____   There's   a _____

Put Your Hand in the Hand

Registration 8
Rhythm: Rock or Jazz Rock

Words and Music by
Gene MacLellan

68

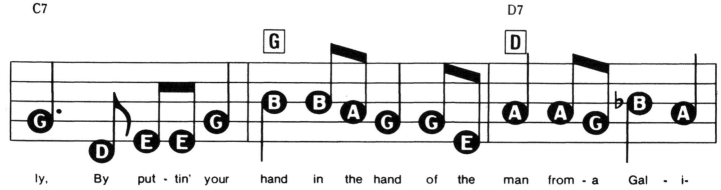

ly, By put-tin' your hand in the hand of the man from - a Gal - i -

lee.

Ev-'ry time I look in - to the
Ma - ma taught me how to pray be - fore I

ho - ly book I wan - na trem - ble. When I
reached the age ____ of ____ sev - en. And when I'm

read a - bout the part where a car - pen - ter cleared ___ the tem - ple
down ___ on my knees that's a when ___ I'm close ___ to heav - en.

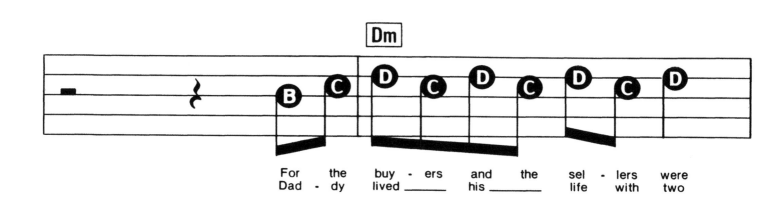

For the buy - ers and the sel - lers were
Dad - dy lived ____ his ____ life with two

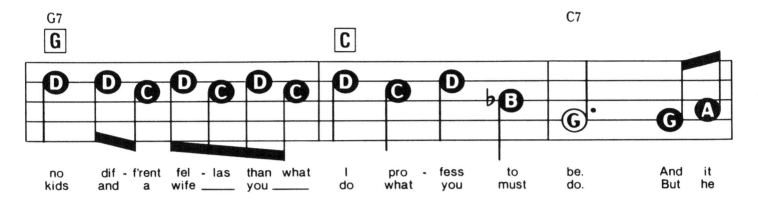

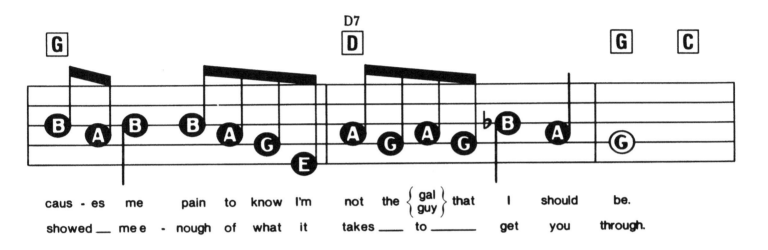

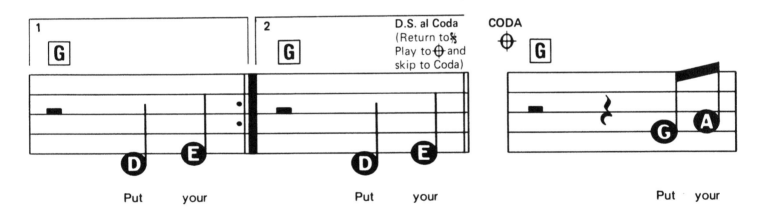

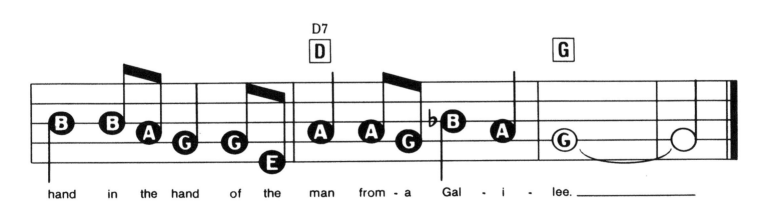

Looking for a City

Registration 8
Rhythm: Fox Trot

Words and Music by Marvin P. Dalton
and Oliver Cooper

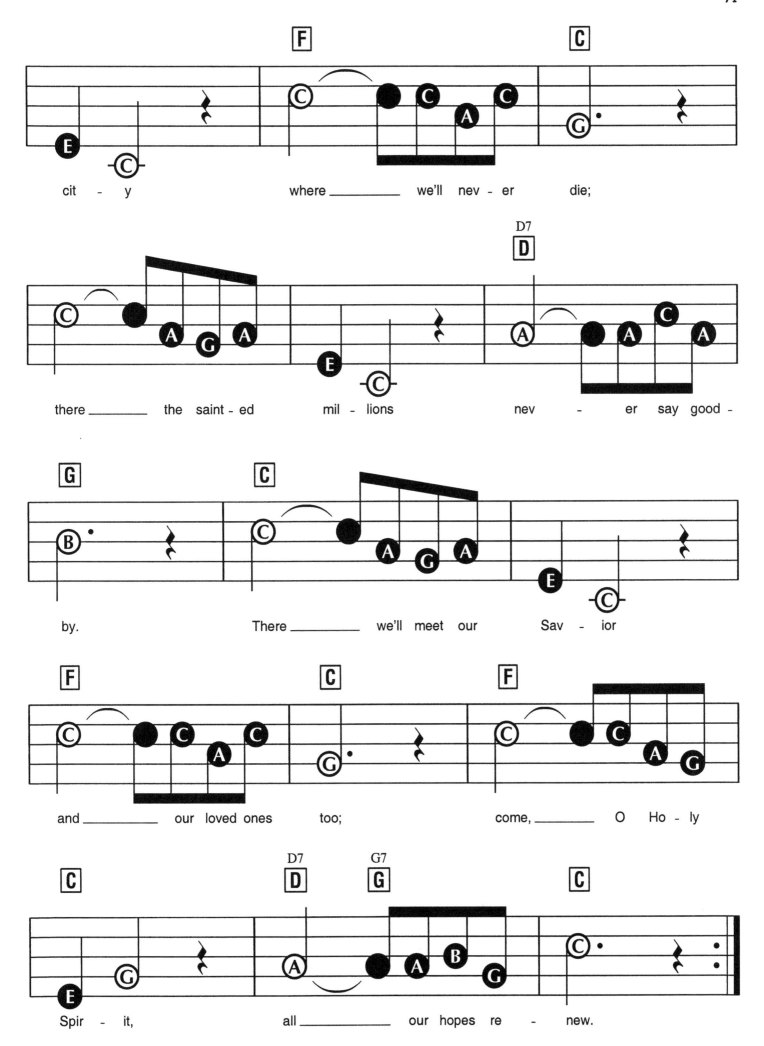

Love Lifted Me

Registration 3
Rhythm: 6/8 March or Waltz

Words by James Rowe
Music by Howard E. Smith

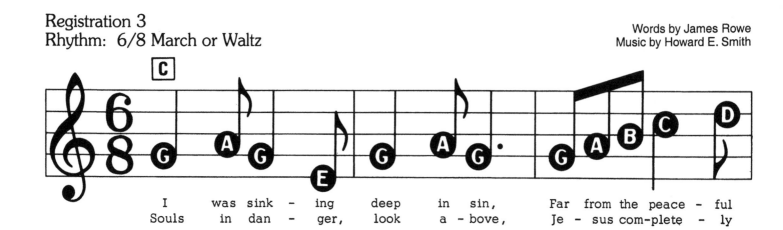

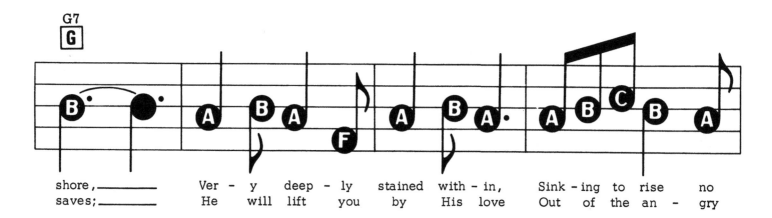

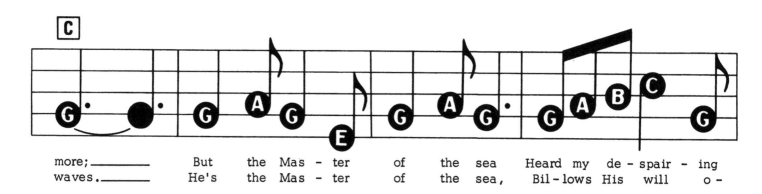

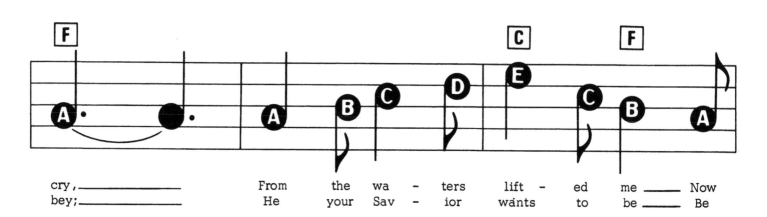

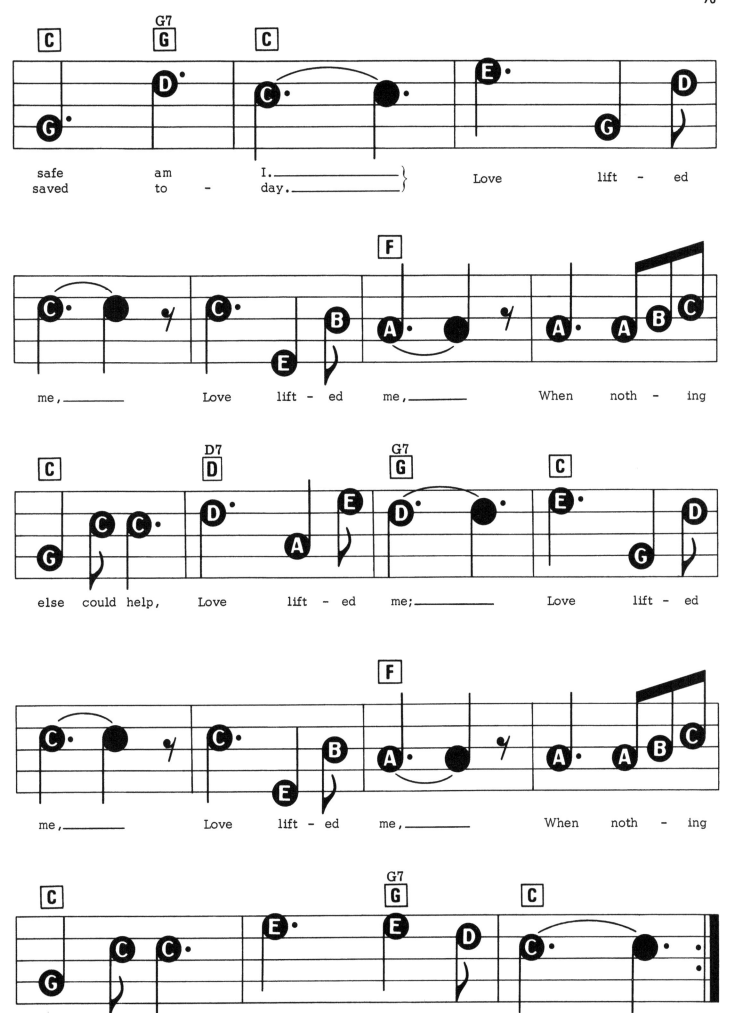

Love Will Roll the Clouds Away

Registration 1
Rhythm: Country or Ballad

Words and Music by
Hale Reeves

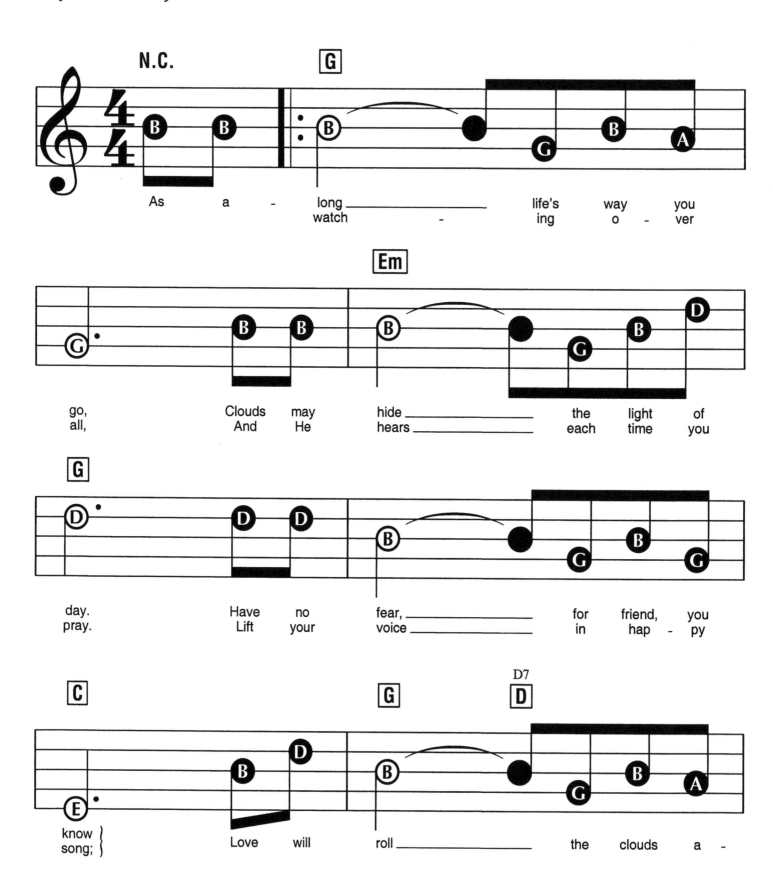

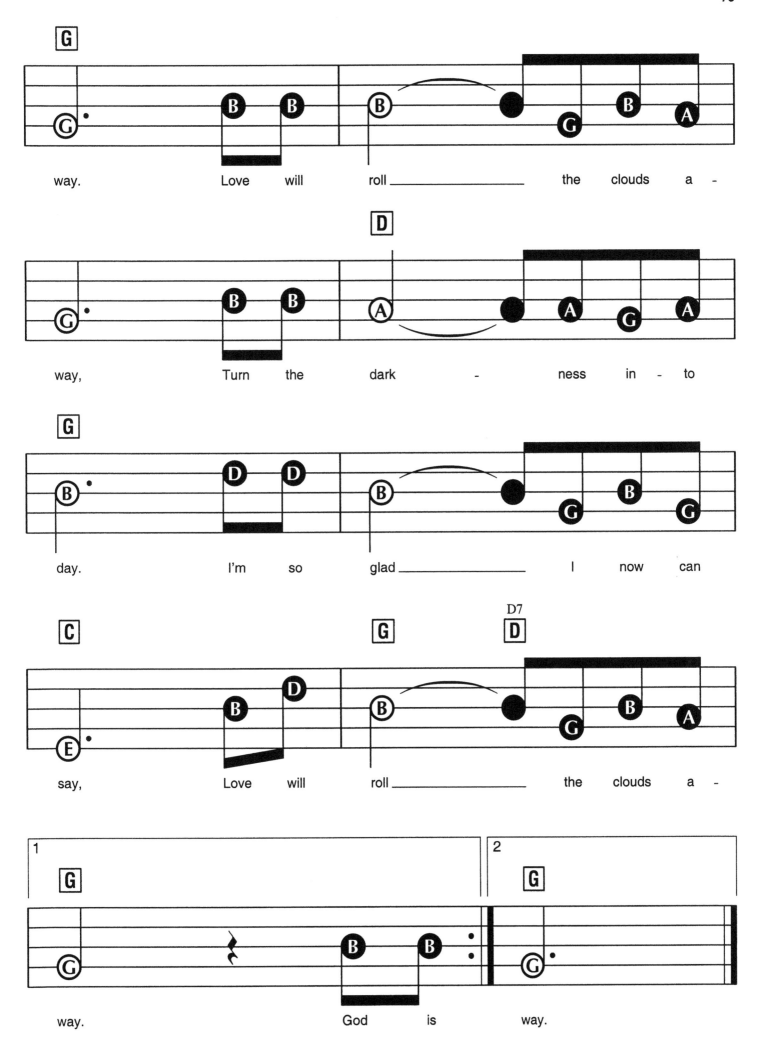

Mansion Over the Hilltop

Registration 5
Rhythm: Swing

Words and Music by
Ira F. Stanphill

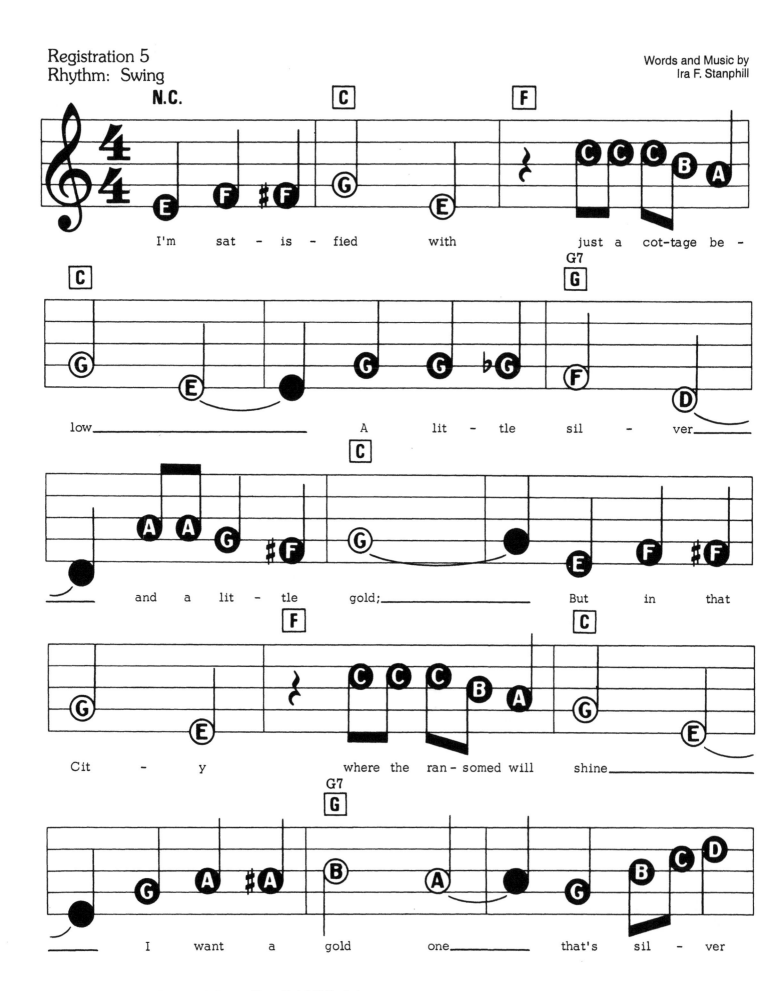

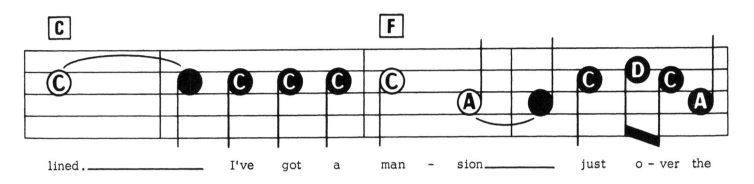

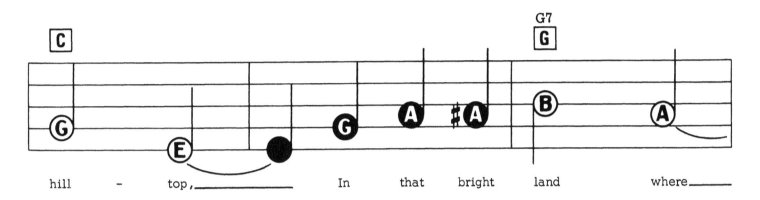

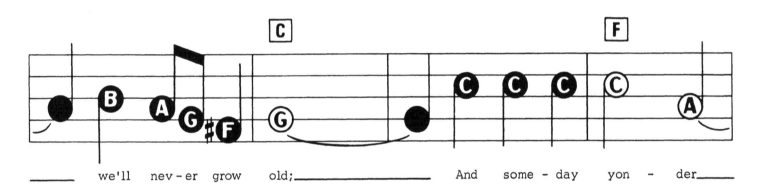

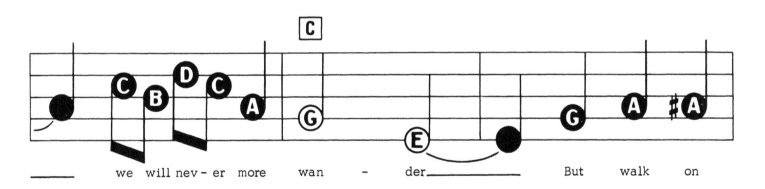

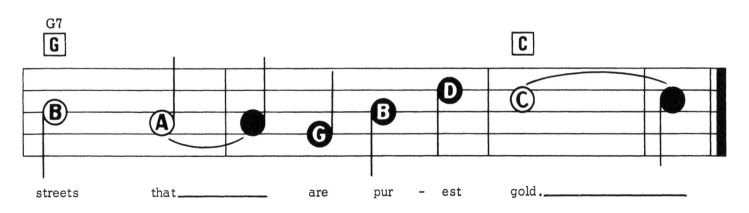

O Come, Angel Band

Registration 1
Rhythm: Waltz

Words by Jefferson Hascall
Music by William B. Bradbury

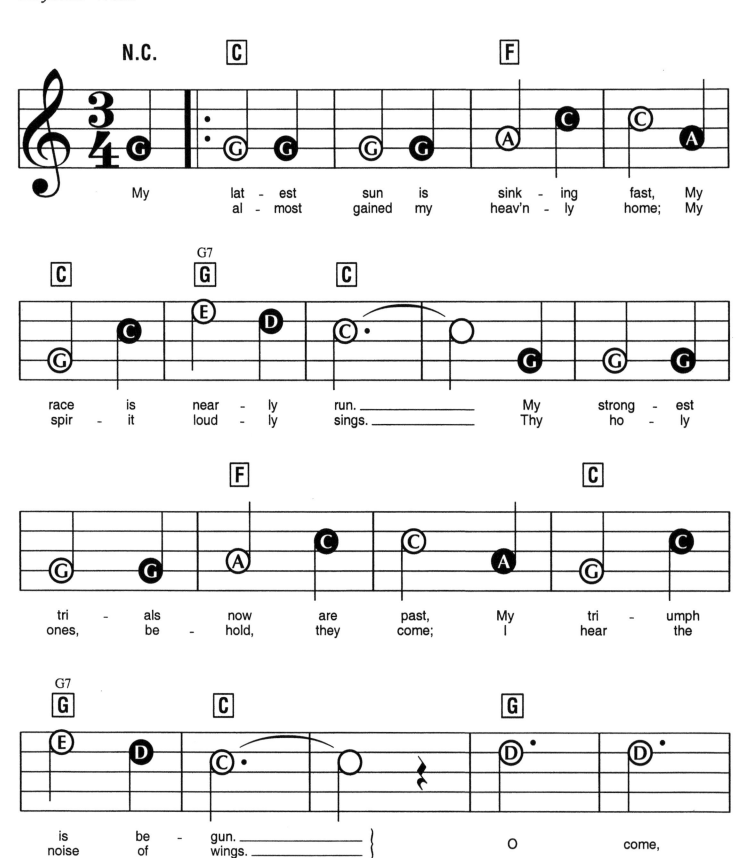

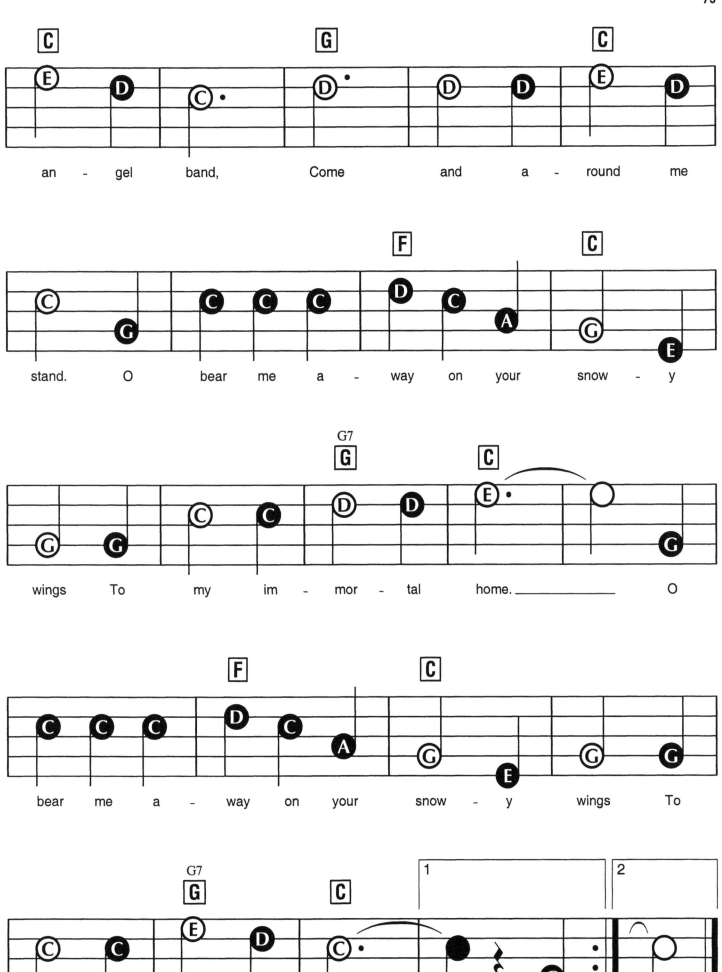

The Old Rugged Cross

Registration 2
Rhythm: Waltz

Words and Music by
Rev. George Bennard

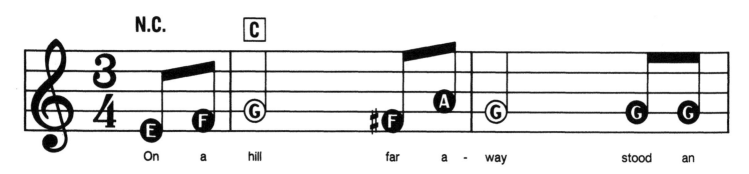

On a hill far a - way stood an

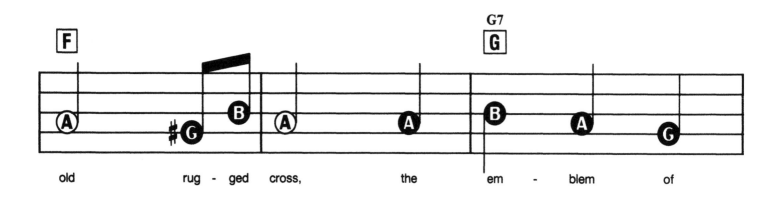

old rug - ged cross, the em - blem of

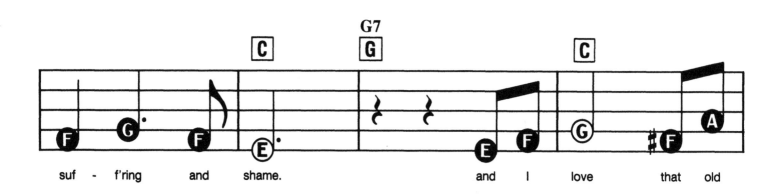

suf - f'ring and shame. and I love that old

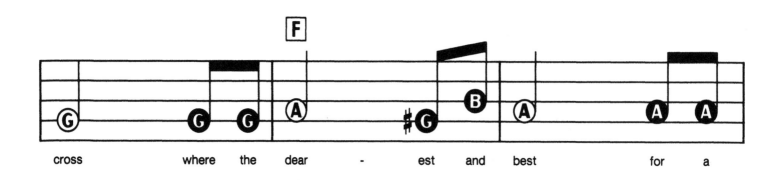

cross where the dear - est and best for a

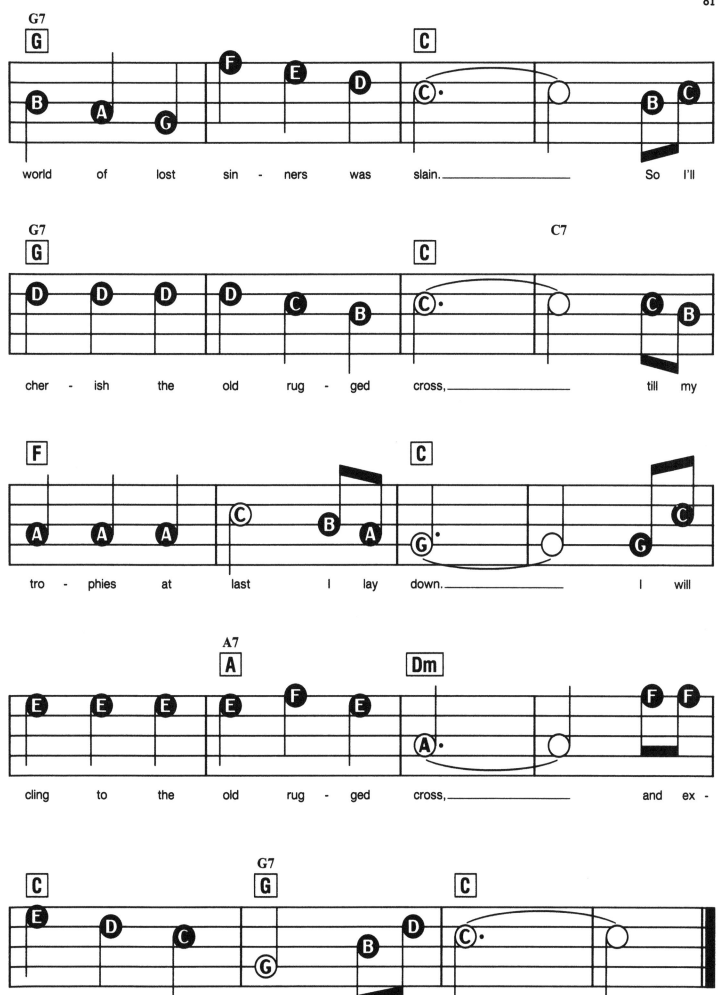

Precious Lord, Take My Hand
(Take My Hand, Precious Lord)

Registration 9
Rhythm: Waltz

Words and Music by
Thomas A. Dorsey

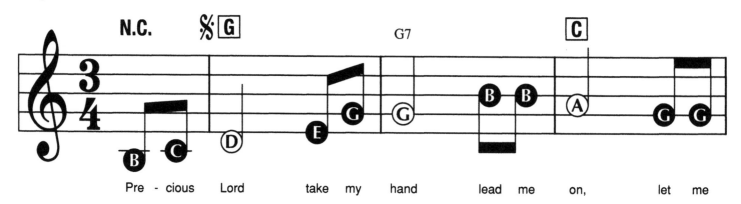

Pre - cious Lord take my hand lead me on, let me

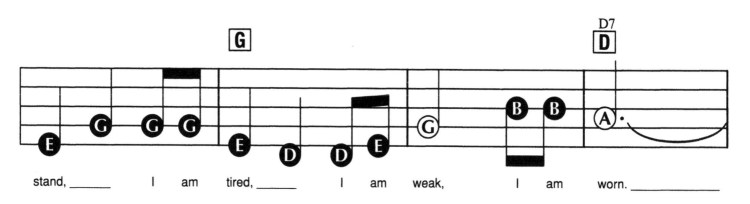

stand, _____ I am tired, _____ I am weak, I am worn. _____

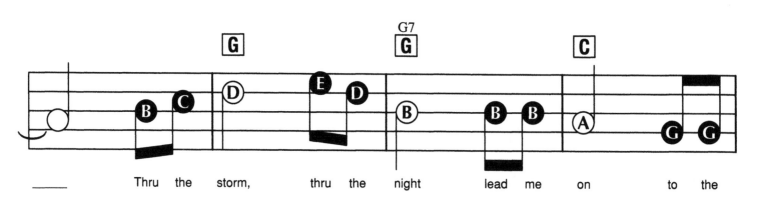

_____ Thru the storm, thru the night lead me on to the

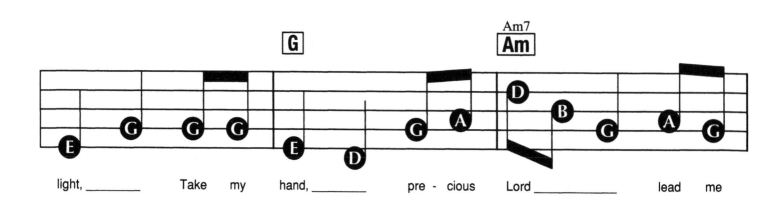

light, _____ Take my hand, _____ pre - cious Lord _____ lead me

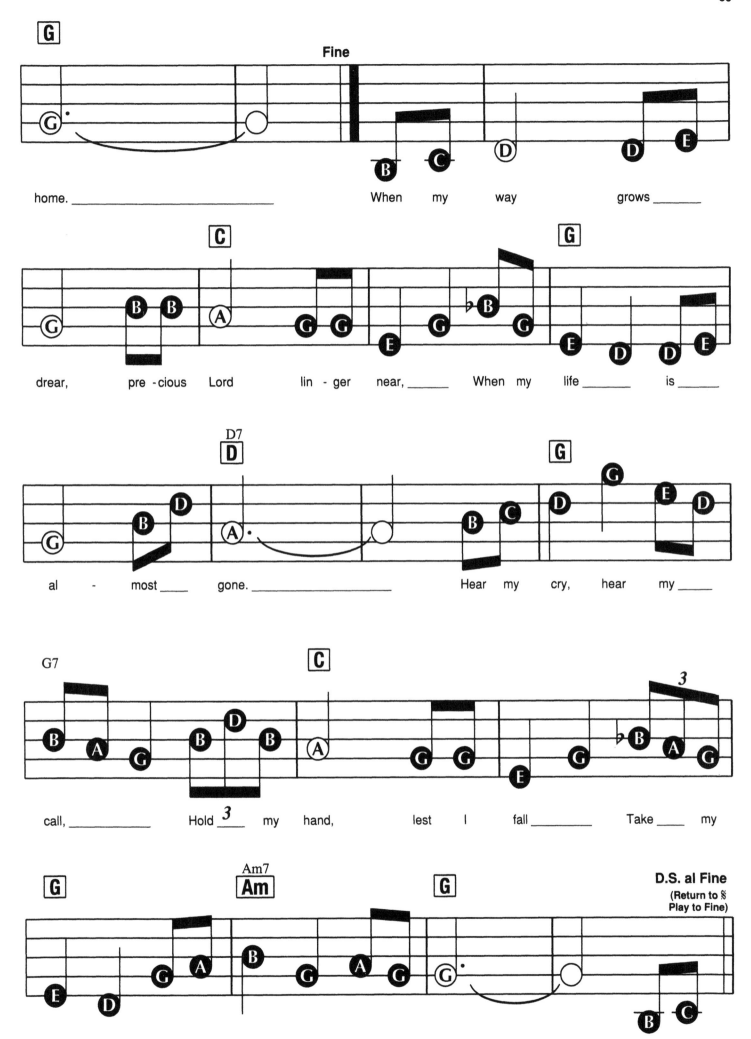

Safely in the Arms of Jesus

Registration 1
Rhythm: Country or Ballad

Words and Music by
Sonny Throckmorton

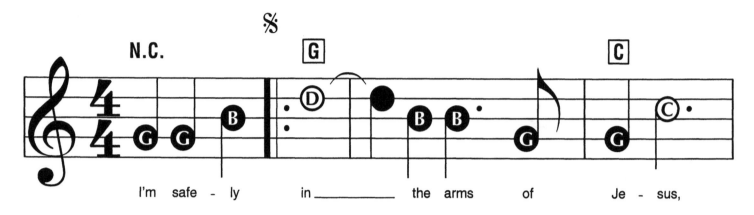

I'm safe - ly in _____ the arms of Je - sus,

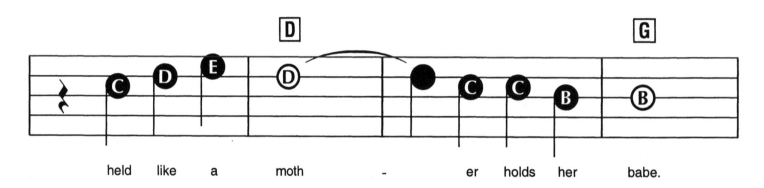

held like a moth - er holds her babe.

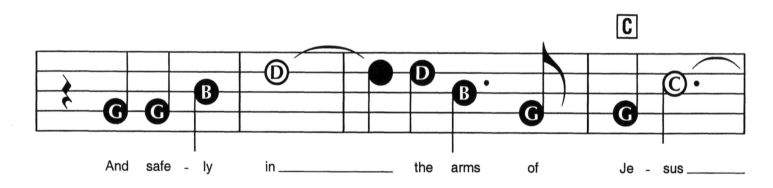

And safe - ly in _____ the arms of Je - sus _____

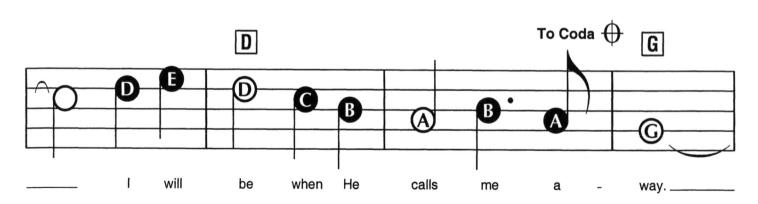

_____ I will be when He calls me a - way. _____

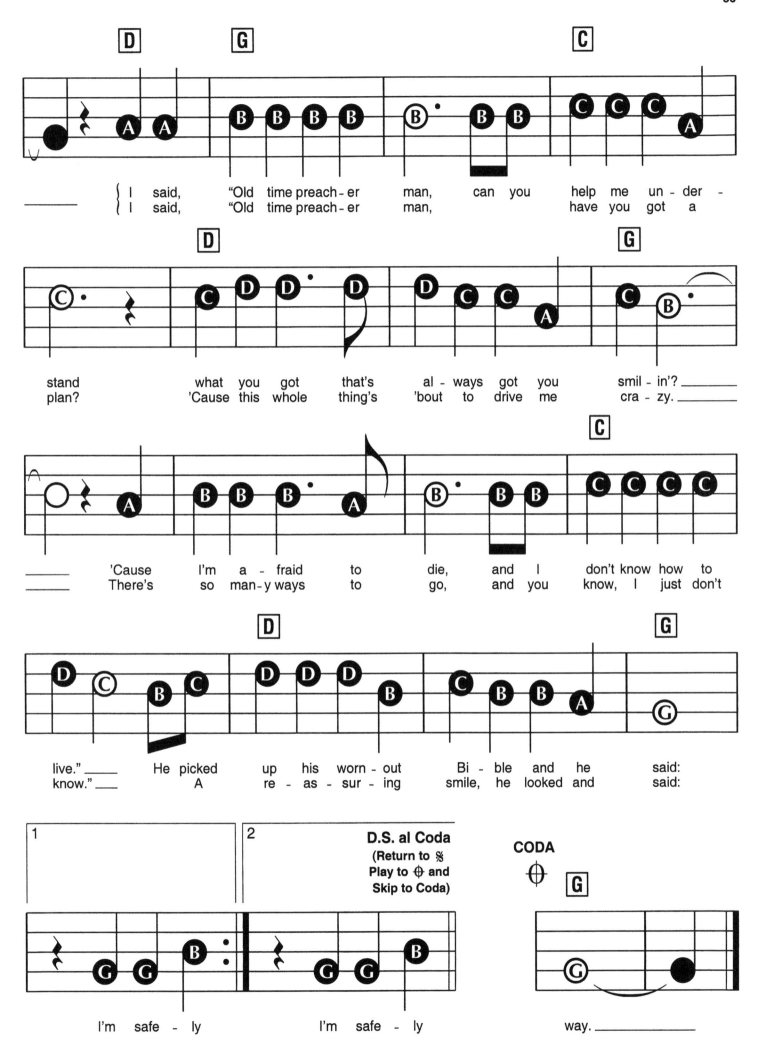

Set Another Place at the Table

Registration 8
Rhythm: Country

Words and Music by Aaron Wilburn,
John Price and John Stalls

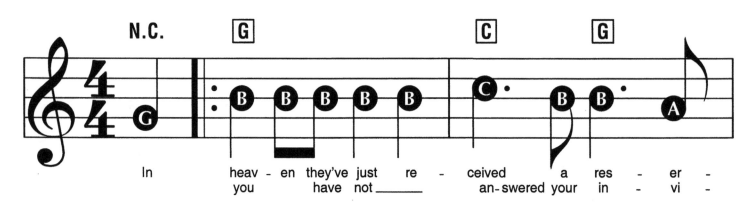

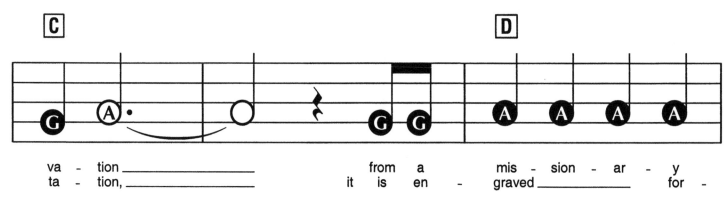

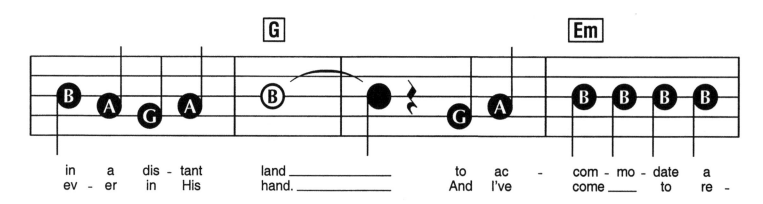

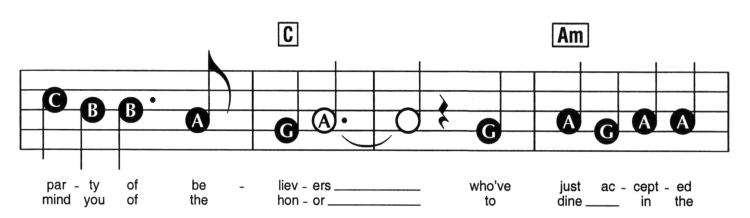

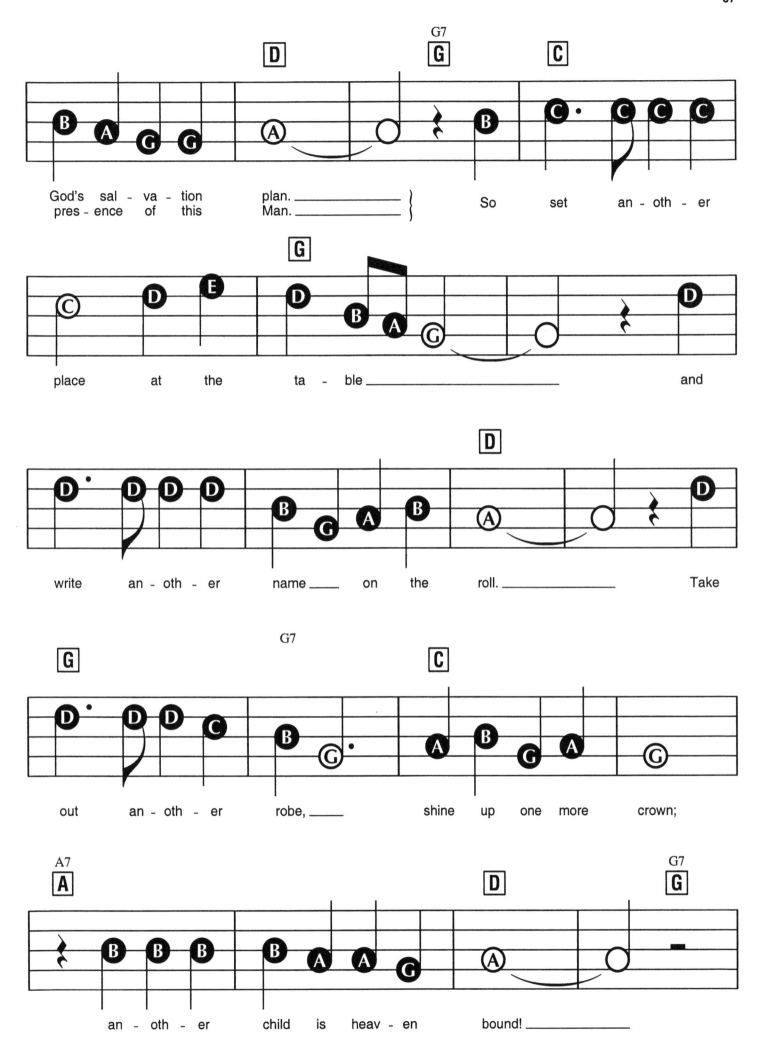

God's sal - va - tion plan. _____
pres - ence of this Man. _____ So set an - oth - er

place at the ta - ble _____ and

write an - oth - er name ____ on the roll. _____ Take

out an - oth - er robe, ____ shine up one more crown;

an - oth - er child is heav - en bound! _____

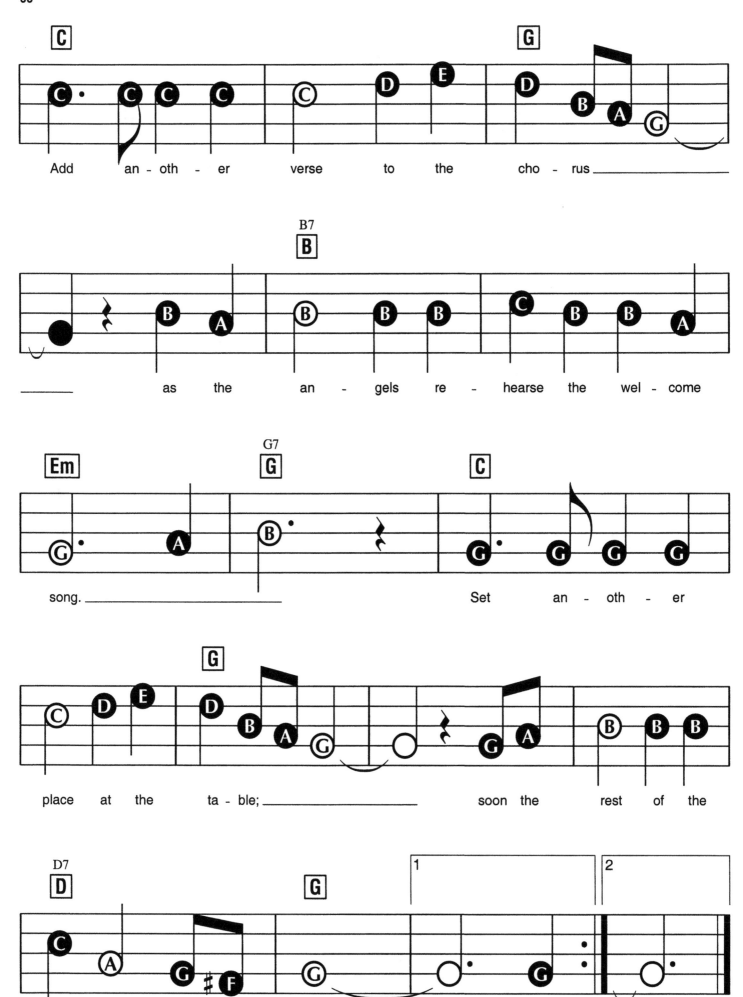

Sheltered in the Arms of God

Registration 8
Rhythm: 4/4 Ballad or Fox Trot

Words and Music by Dottie Rambo
and Jimmie Davis

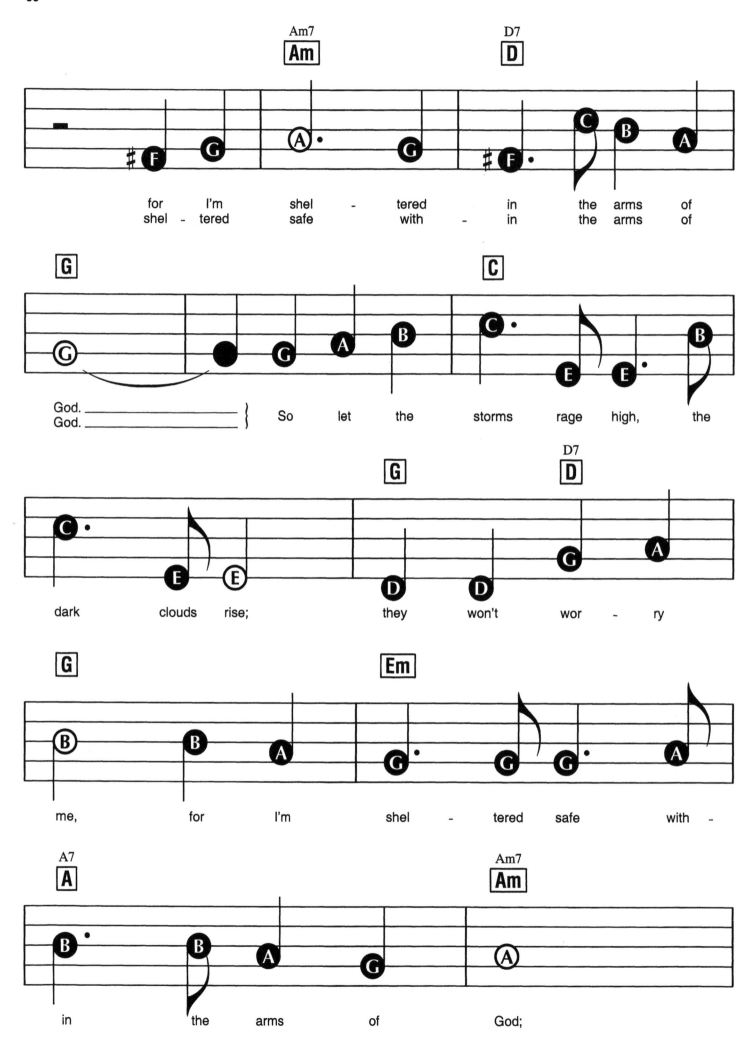

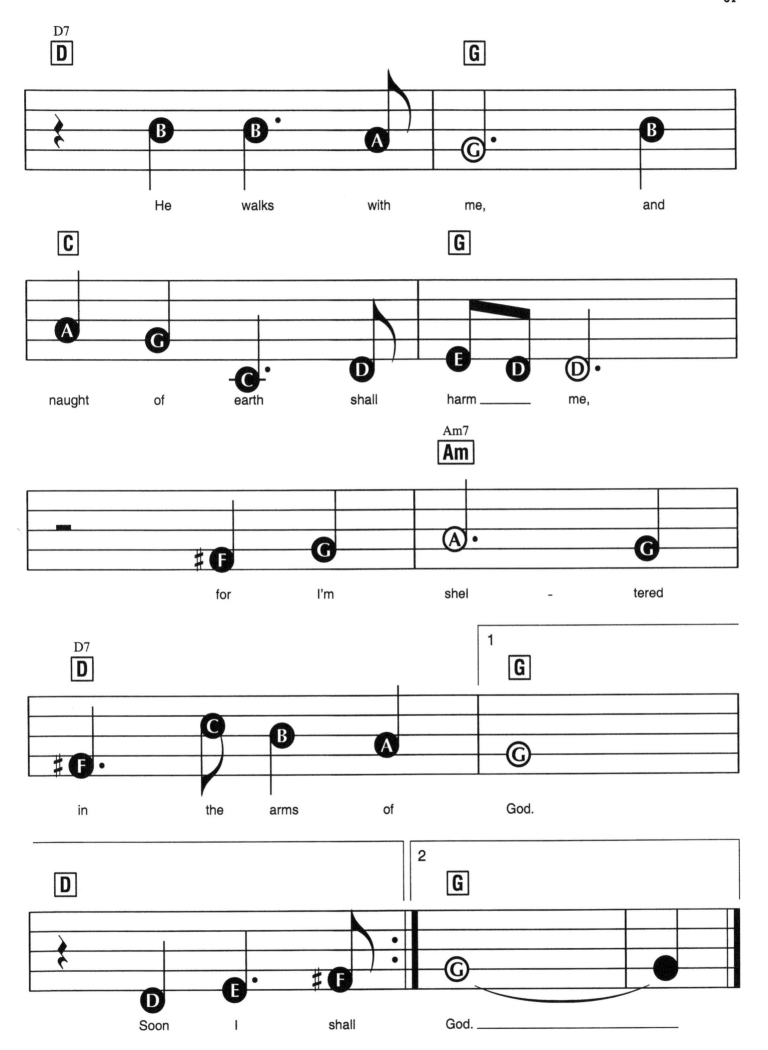

Suppertime

Registration 5
Rhythm: Swing

Words and Music by
Ira F. Stanphill

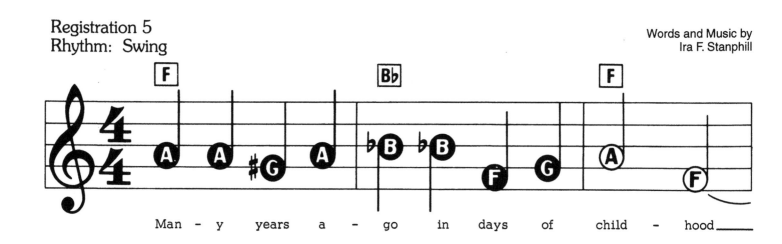

Man - y years a - go in days of child - hood___

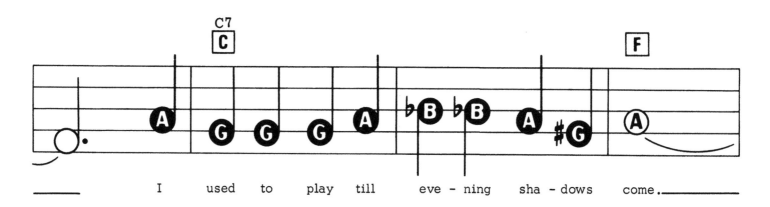

___ I used to play till eve - ning sha - dows come.___

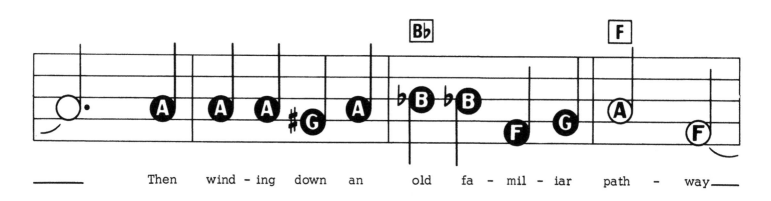

___ Then wind - ing down an old fa - mil - iar path - way___

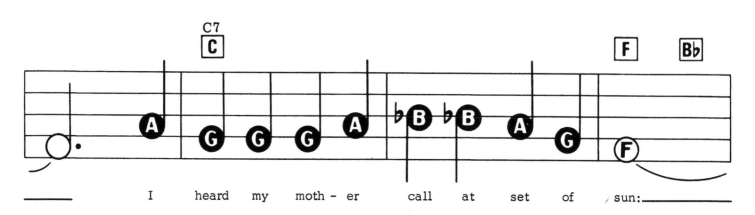

___ I heard my moth - er call at set of sun:___

93

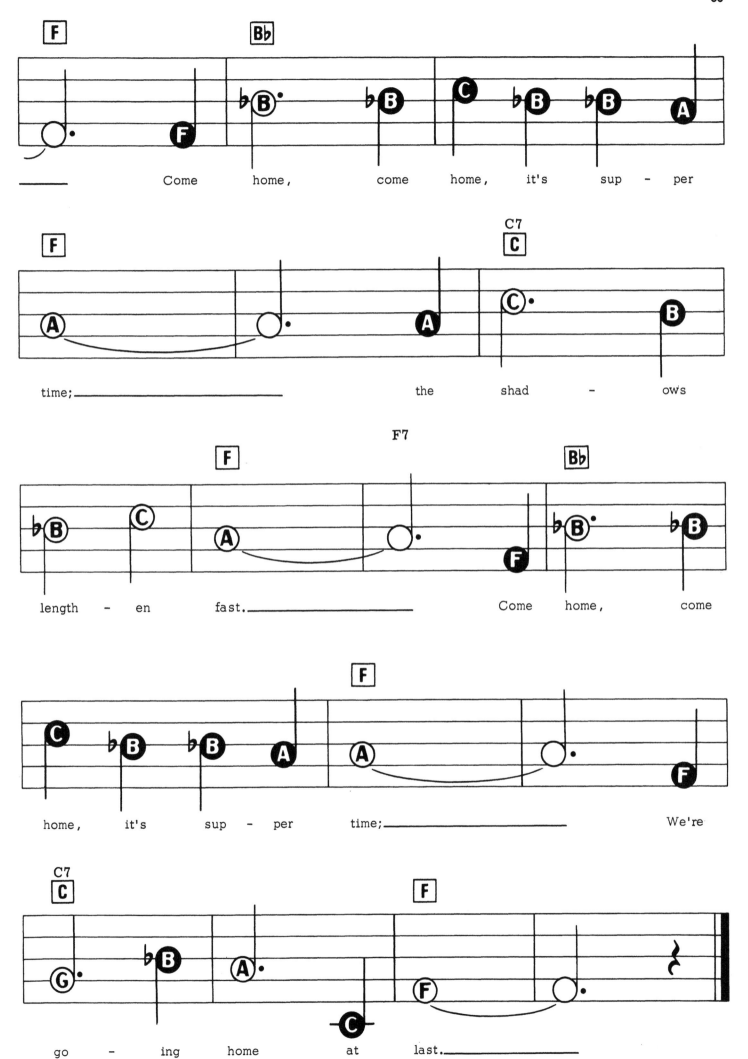

That's the Man I'm Looking For

Registration 3
Rhythm: Country or Fox Trot

Words and Music by
Don Lee

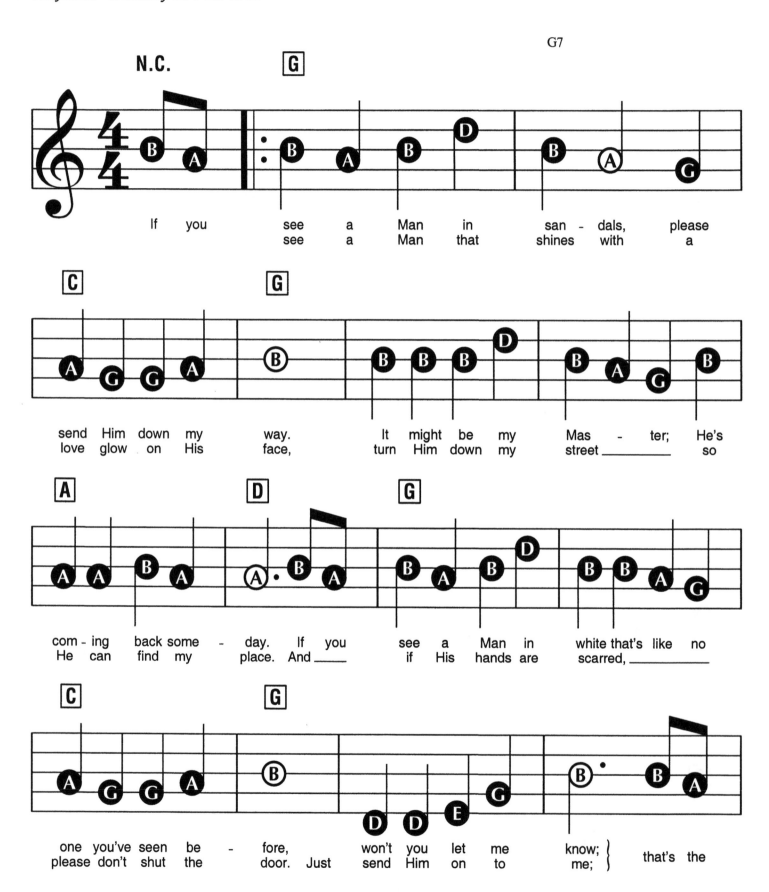

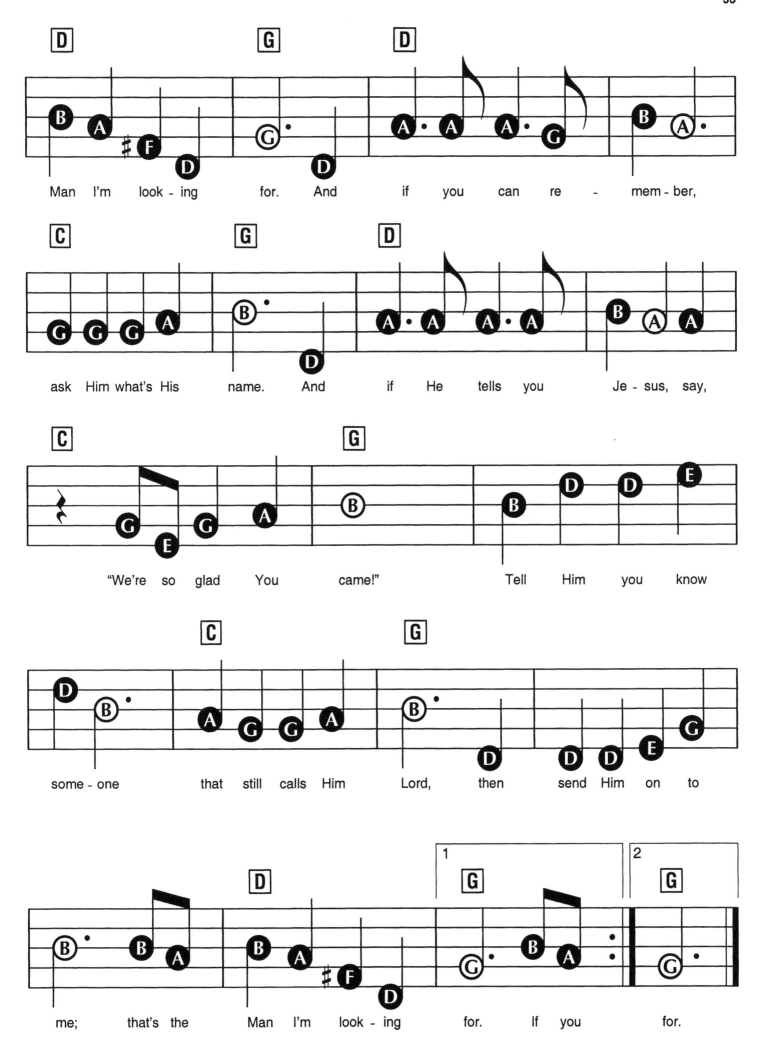

This Is Just What Heaven Means to Me

Registration 4
Rhythm: Country or Ballad

Traditional

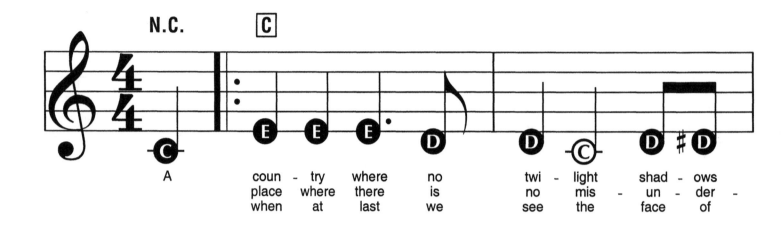

A
coun - try where no twi - light shad - ows
place where there is no mis - un - der -
when at last we see the face of

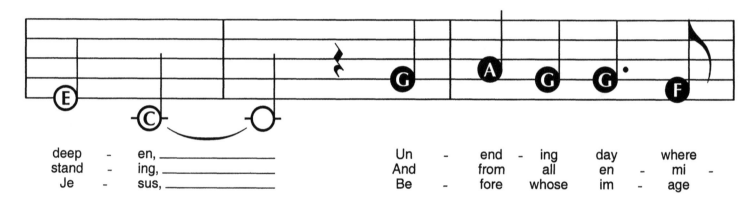

deep - en, _____
stand - ing, _____
Je - sus, _____

Un - end - ing day where
And from all en - mi
Be - fore whose im - age

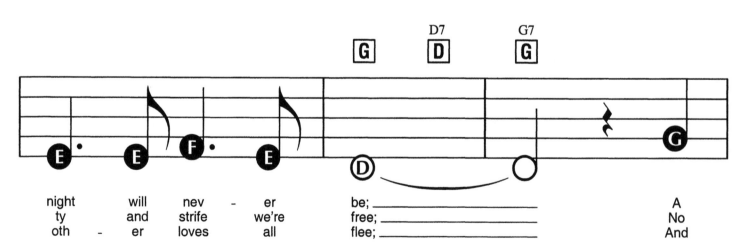

night will nev - er be; _____ A
ty and strife we're free; _____ No
oth - er loves all flee; _____ And

97

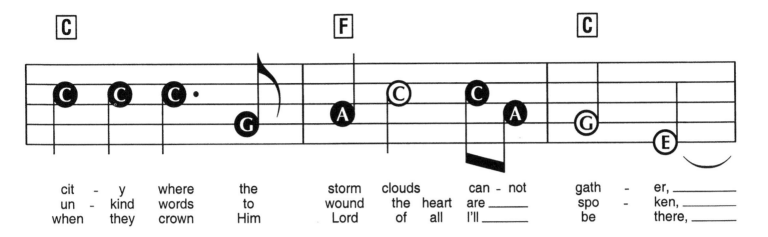

cit - y where the storm clouds can - not gath - er, _____
un - kind where words to wound the heart are _____ spo - ken, _____
when they crown to Him Lord of all I'll _____ be there, _____

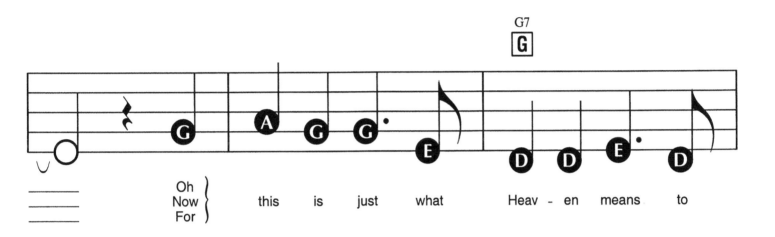

_____ Oh this is just what Heav - en means to
Now
For

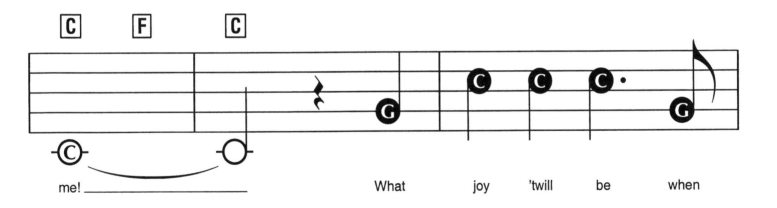

me! _____ What joy 'twill be when

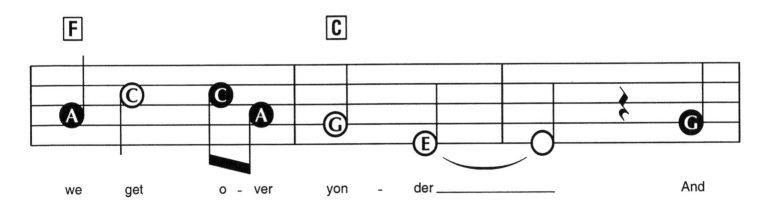

we get o - ver yon - der _____ And

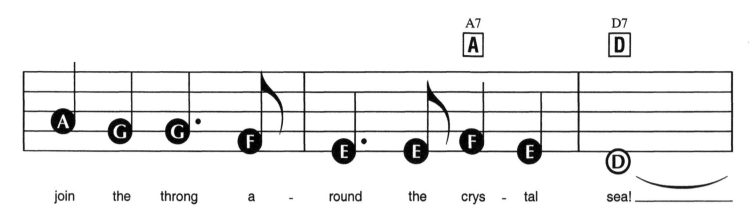

join the throng a - round the crys - tal sea! _____

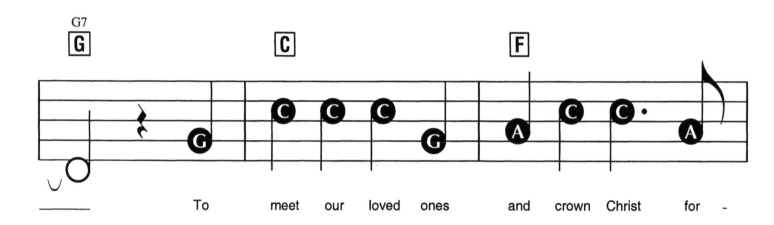

_____ To meet our loved ones and crown Christ for -

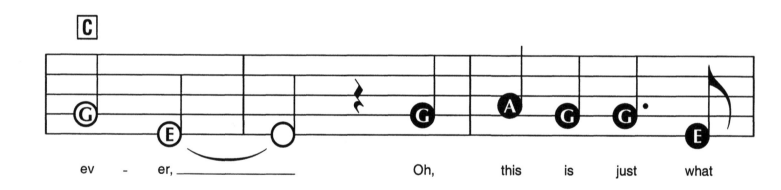

ev - er, _____ Oh, this is just what

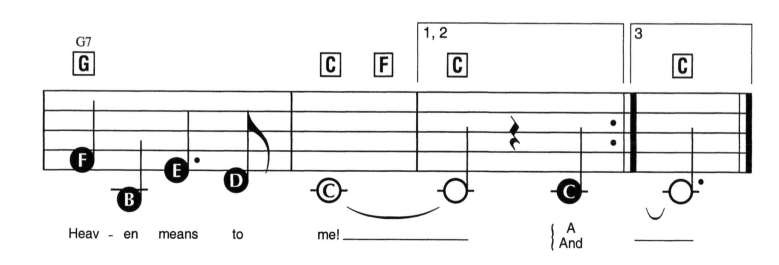

Heav - en means to me! _____ { A / And } _____

Turn Your Radio On

Registration 2
Rhythm: Rock

Words and Music by
Albert E. Brumley

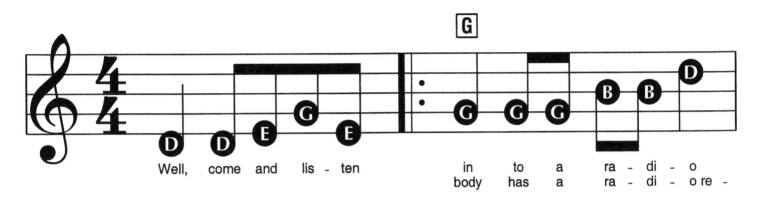

Well, come and lis - ten in to a ra - di - o
body has a ra - di - o re -

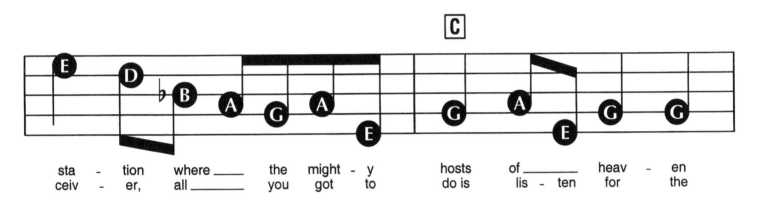

sta - tion where ___ the might - y hosts of ___ heav - en
ceiv - er, all ___ you got to do is lis - ten for the

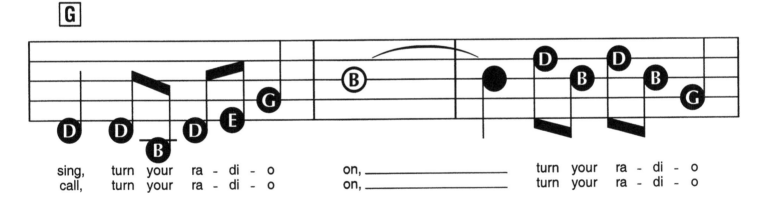

sing, turn your ra - di - o on, ___ turn your ra - di - o
call, turn your ra - di - o on, ___ turn your ra - di - o

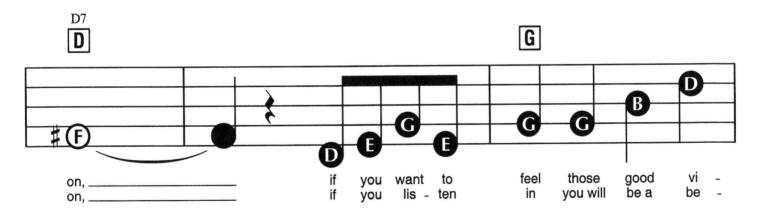

on, ___ if you want to feel those good vi -
on, ___ if you lis - ten in you will be a be -

101

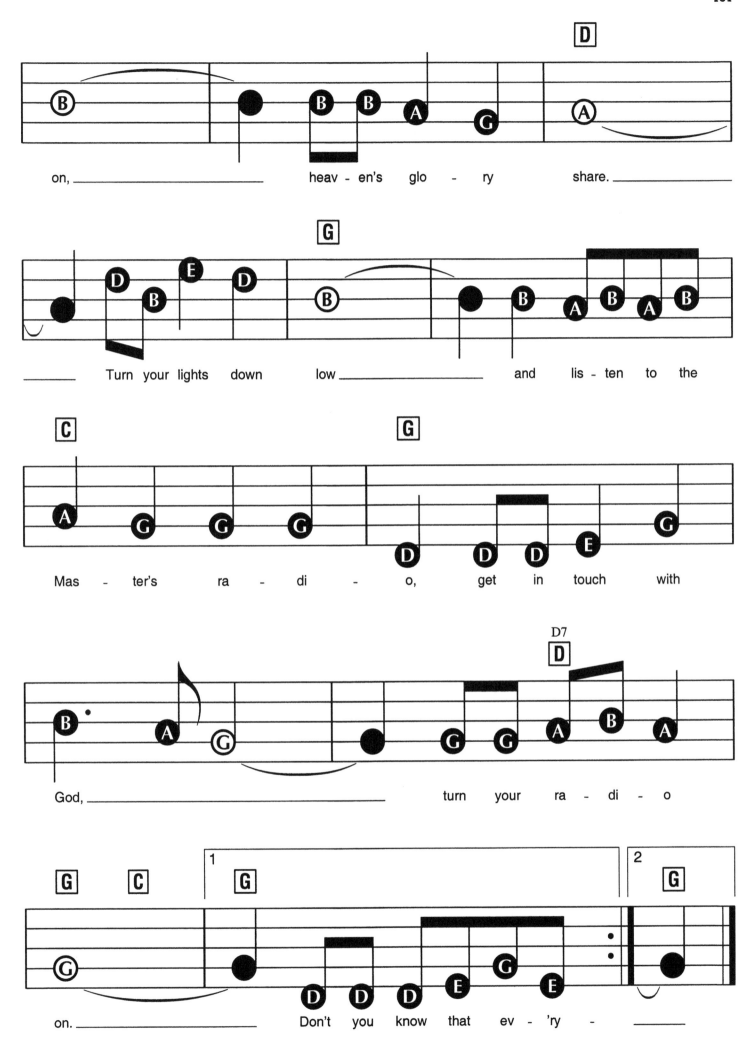

The Unclouded Day

Registration 8
Rhythm: Bluegrass

Words and Music by
J.K. Alwood

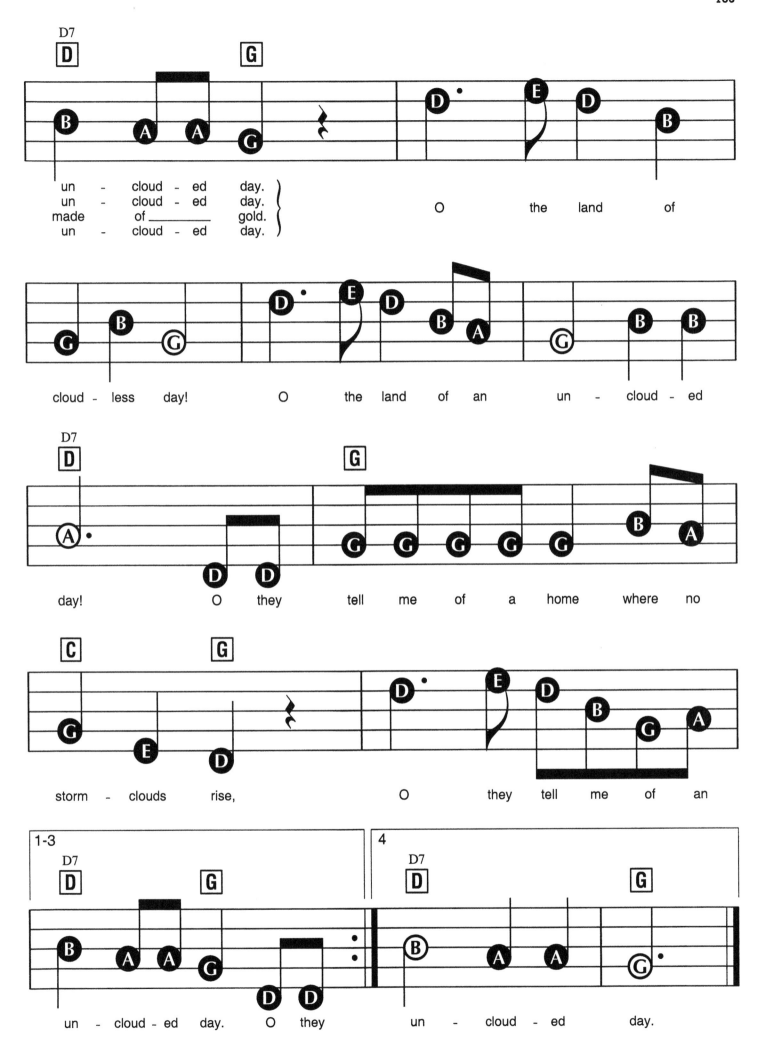

Wayfaring Stranger

Registration 8
Rhythm: Swing

Southern American Folk Hymn

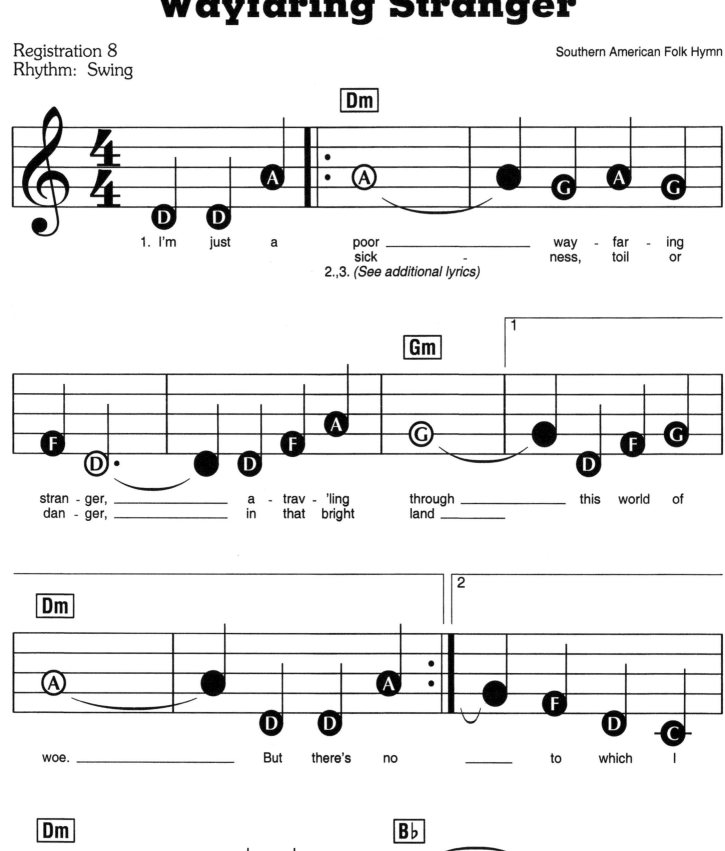

1. I'm just a poor _____ way - far - ing
   sick - ness, toil or
2.,3. *(See additional lyrics)*

stran - ger, _____ a - trav - 'ling through _____ this world of
dan - ger, _____ in that bright land _____

woe. _____ But there's no _____ to which I

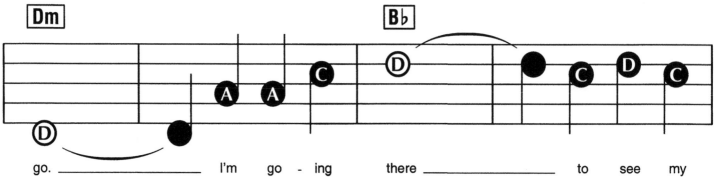

go. _____ I'm go - ing there _____ to see my

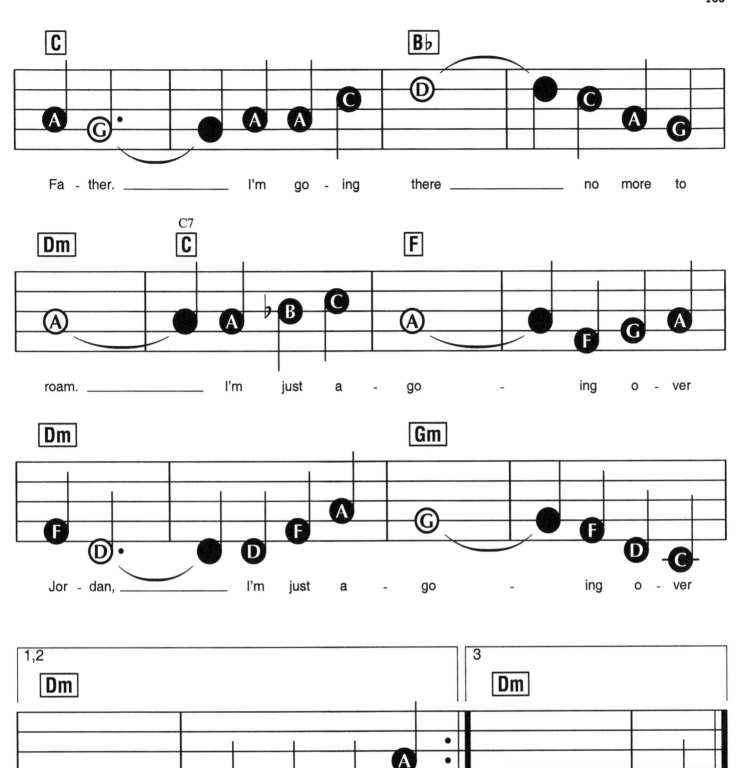

Additional Lyrics

2. I know dark clouds will gather 'round me,
   I know my way is steep and rough.
   But beauteous fields lie just beyond me
   Where souls redeemed their vigil keep.
   I'm going there to meet my mother,
   She said she'd meet me when I come...

3. I want to wear a crown of glory
   When I get home to that bright land.
   I want to shout Salvation's story,
   In concert with that bloodwashed band.
   I'm going there to meet my Saviour,
   To sing His praise forever more...

When the Book of Life Is Read

Registration 9
Rhythm: Fox Trot

Words and Music by
Hank Williams

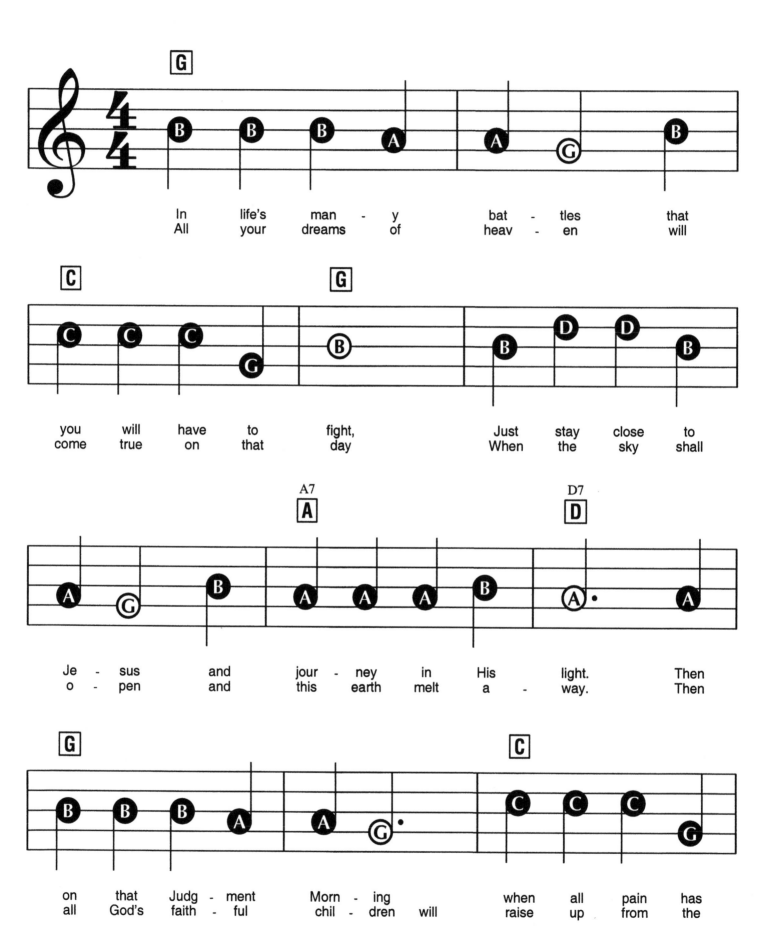

107

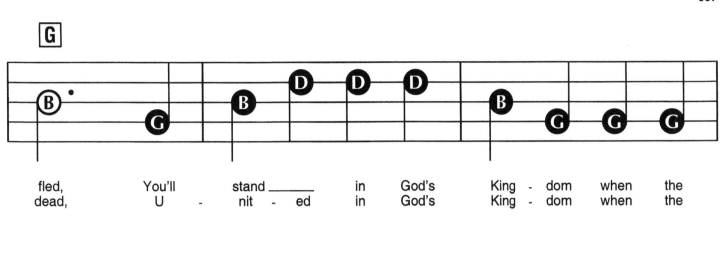

fled, You'll stand _____ in God's King - dom when the
dead, U - nit - ed in God's King - dom when the

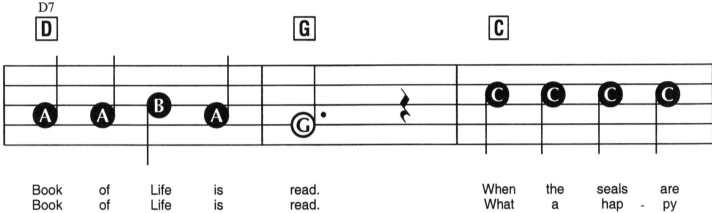

Book of Life is read. When the seals are
Book of Life is read. What a hap - py

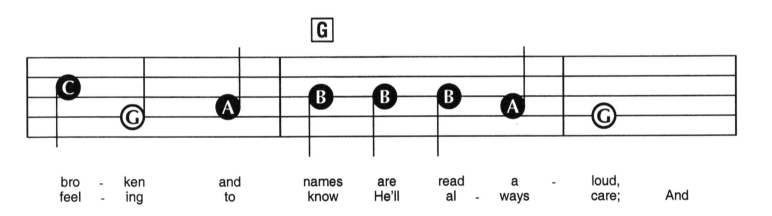

bro - ken and names are read a - loud,
feel - ing to know He'll al - ways care; And

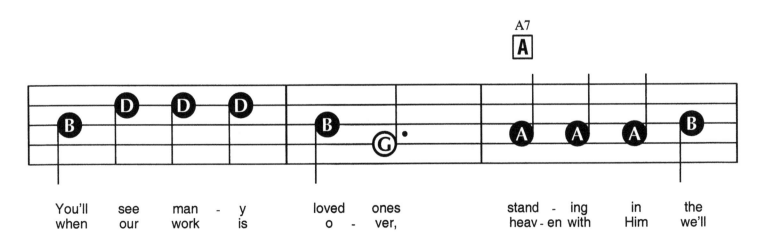

You'll see man - y loved ones stand - ing in the
when our work is o - ver, heav - en with Him we'll

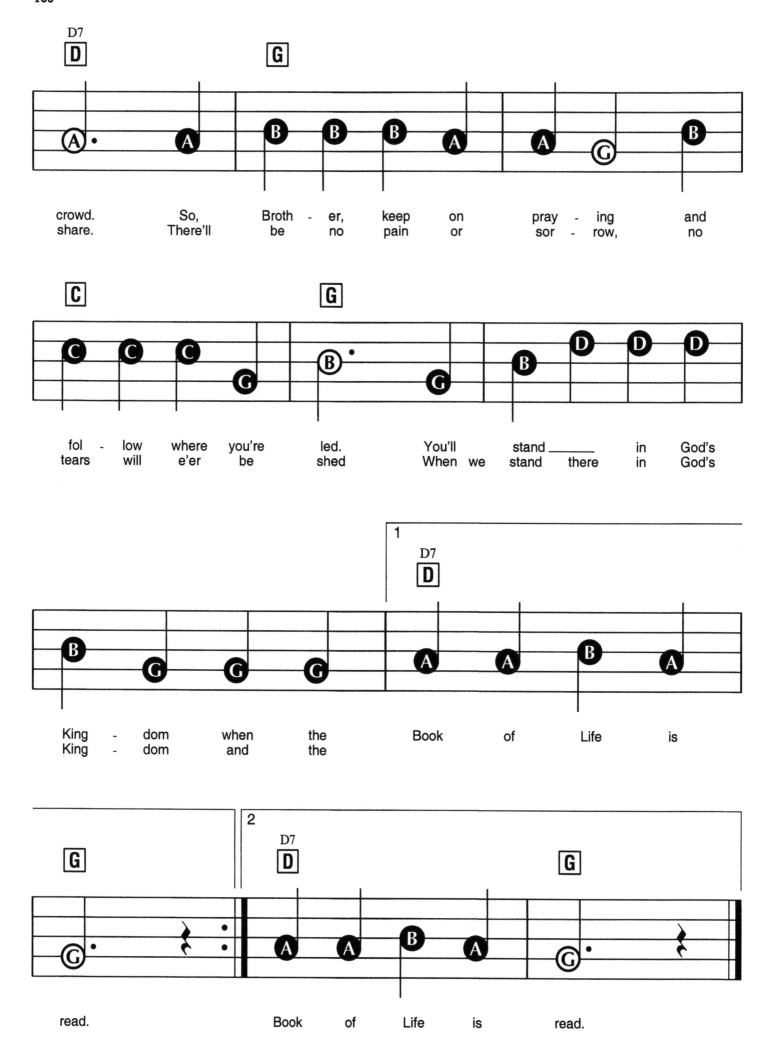

When the Saints Go Marching In

Registration 2
Rhythm: Swing

Words by Katherine E. Purvis
Music by James M. Black

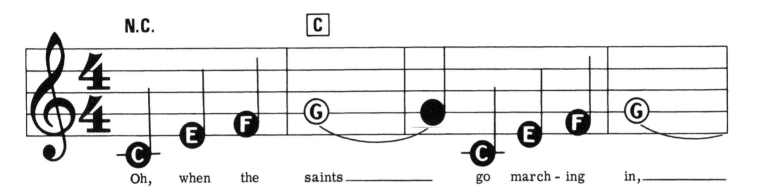

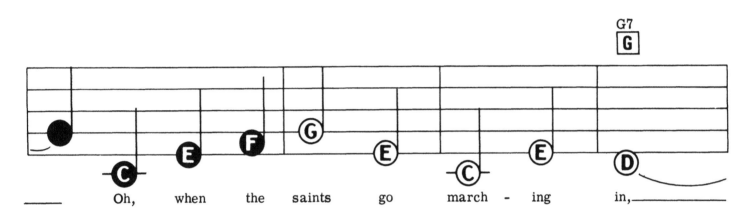

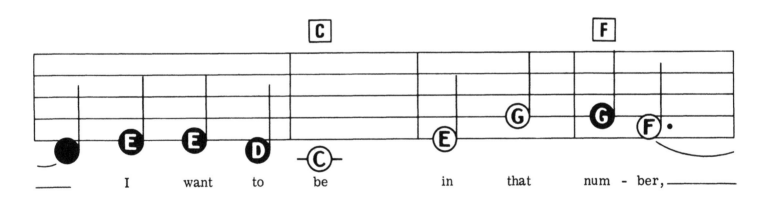

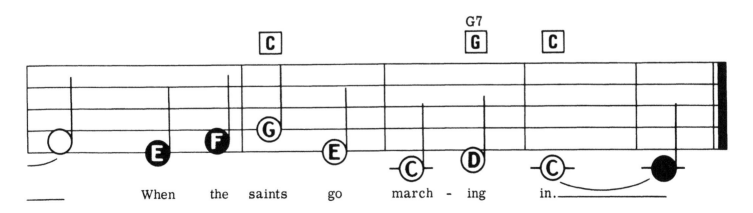

When We All Get to Heaven

Registration 4
Rhythm: Ballad or Fox Trot

Words by Eliza E. Hewitt
Music by Emily D. Wilson

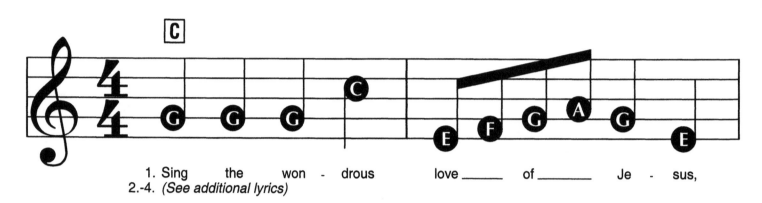

1. Sing the won - drous love _____ of _____ Je - sus,
2.-4. *(See additional lyrics)*

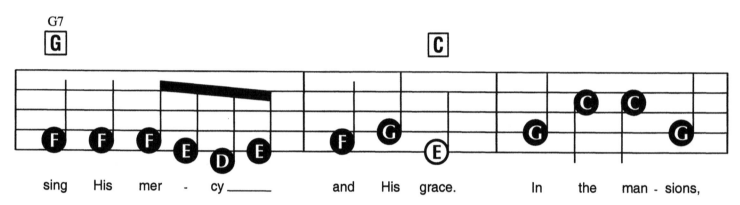

sing His mer - cy _____ and His grace. In the man - sions,

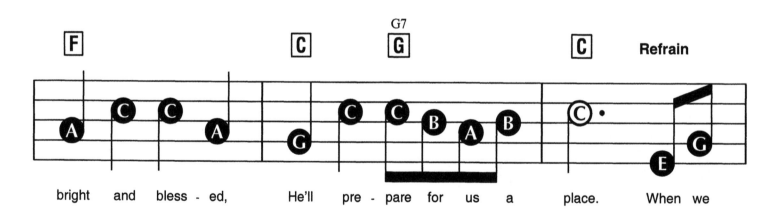

bright and bless - ed, He'll pre - pare for us a place. When we

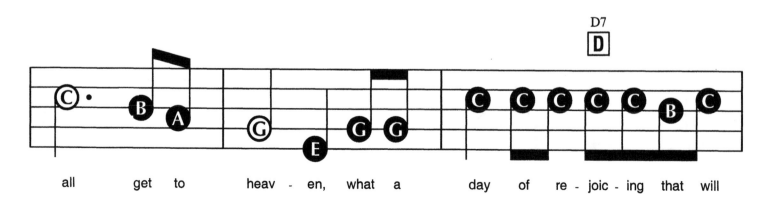

all get to heav - en, what a day of re - joic - ing that will

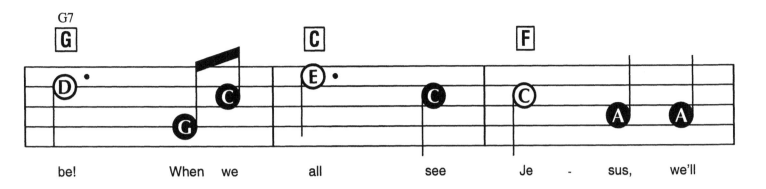

be! When we all see Je - sus, we'll

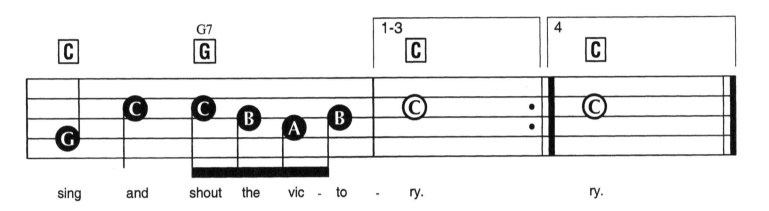

sing and shout the vic - to - ry. ry.

Additional Lyrics

2. While we walk the pilgrim pathway,
   Clouds will overspread the sky;
   But when trav'ling days are over,
   Not a shadow, not a sigh!
   Refrain

3. Let us then be true and faithful,
   Trusting, serving ev'ryday.
   Just one glimpse of Him in glory
   Will the toils of life repay.
   Refrain

4. Onward to the prize before us!
   Soon His beauty we'll behold.
   Soon the pearly gates will open;
   We shall tread the streets of gold.
   Refrain

Why Me?
(Why Me, Lord?)

Registration 4
Rhythm: Waltz

Words and Music by
Kris Kristofferson

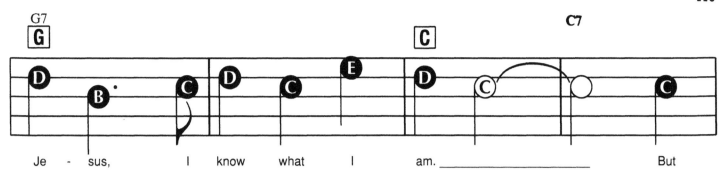

Je - sus, I know what I am. _____ But

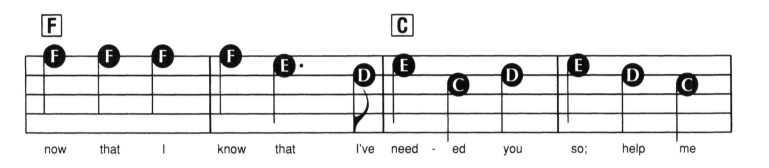

now that I know that I've need - ed you so; help me

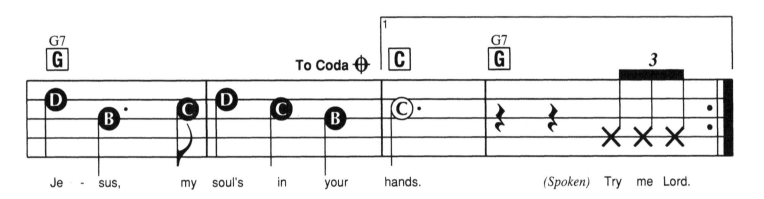

Je - sus, my soul's in your hands. *(Spoken)* Try me Lord.

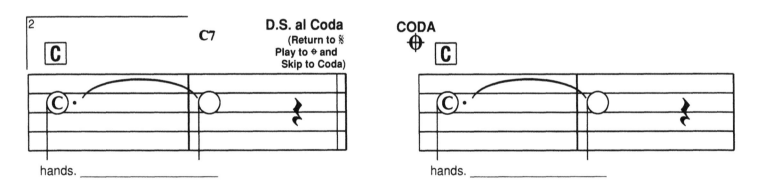

hands. _____

hands. _____

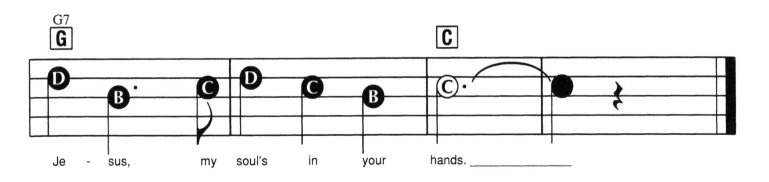

Je - sus, my soul's in your hands. _____

Will the Circle Be Unbroken

Registration 4
Rhythm: Swing

Words by Ada R. Habershon
Music by Charles H. Gabriel

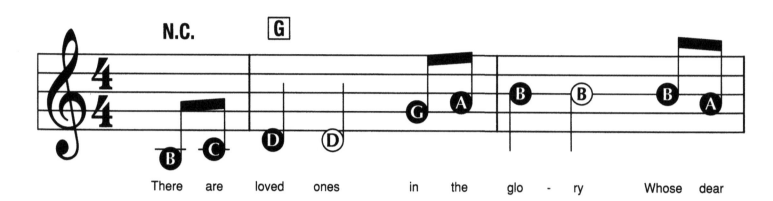

There are loved ones in the glo - ry Whose dear

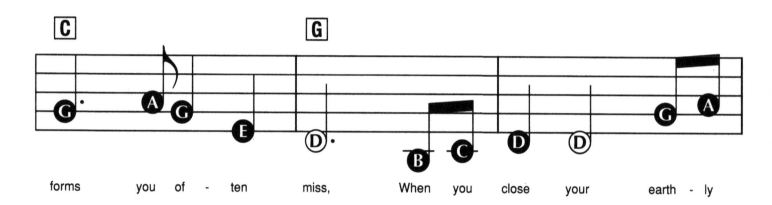

forms you of - ten miss, When you close your earth - ly

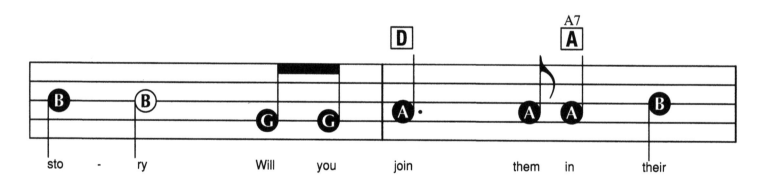

sto - ry Will you join them in their

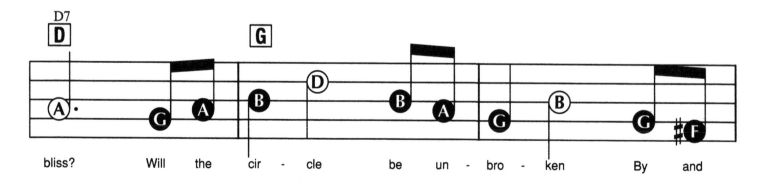

bliss? Will the cir - cle be un - bro - ken By and

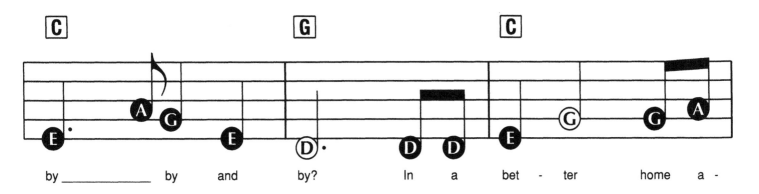

by _____ by and by? In a bet - ter home a -

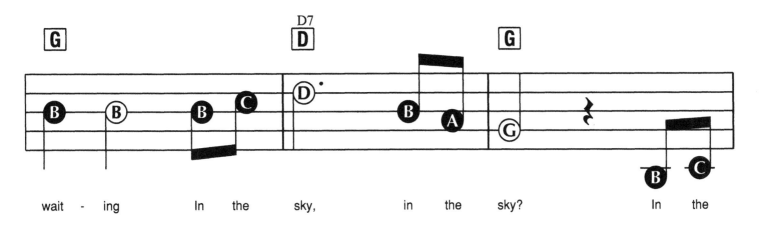

wait - ing In the sky, in the sky? In the

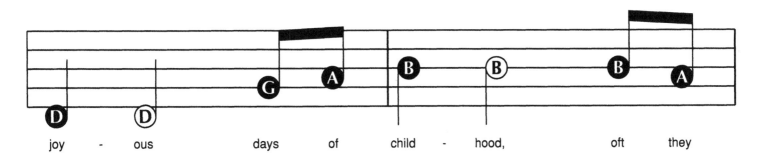

joy - ous days of child - hood, oft they

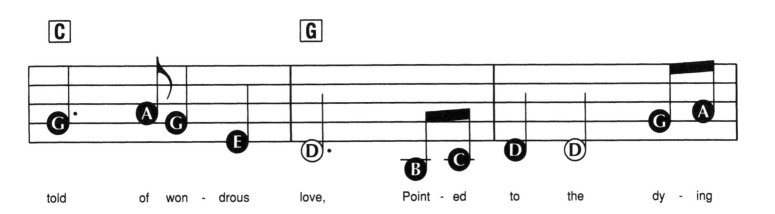

told of won - drous love, Point - ed to the dy - ing

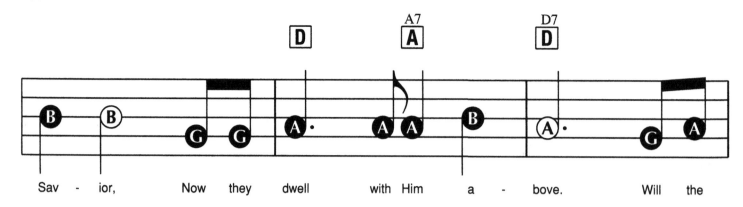

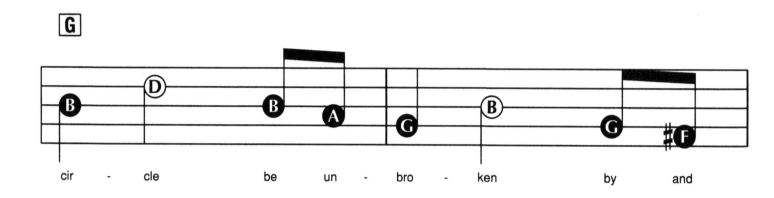

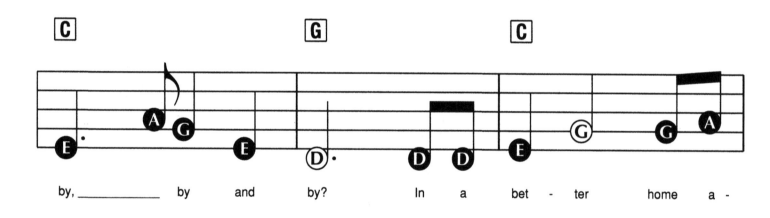

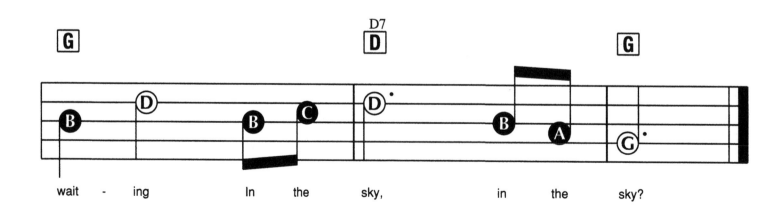

You Make It Rain for Me

Registration 1
Rhythm: Ballad

Words and Music by
Larry Stallings

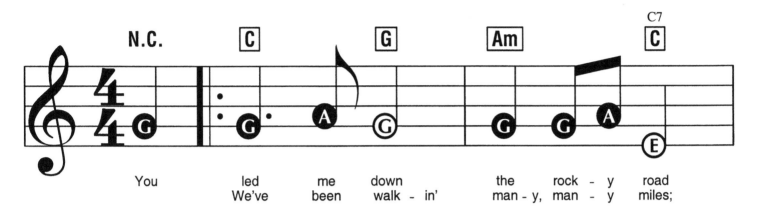

You led me down the rock - y road
We've been walk - in' man - y, man - y miles;

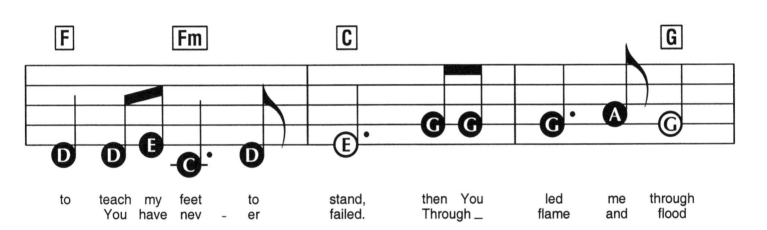

to teach my feet to stand, then You led me through
You have nev - er failed. Through _ flame and through flood

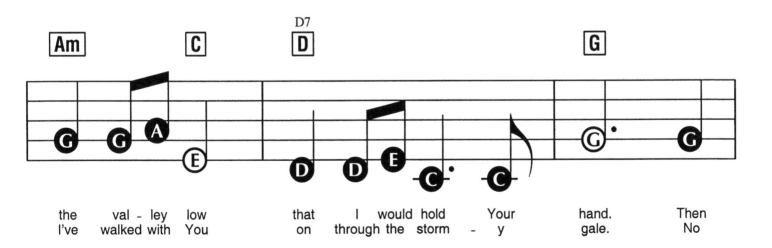

the val - ley low that I would hold Your hand. Then
I've walked with You on through the storm - y gale. No

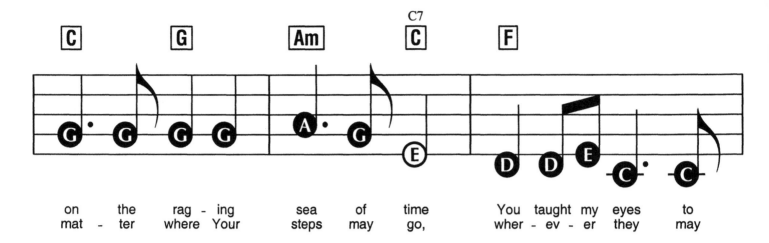

on the   rag - ing   sea   of   time
mat - ter   where Your   steps   may   go,   You   taught   my   eyes   to
wher - ev - er   they   may

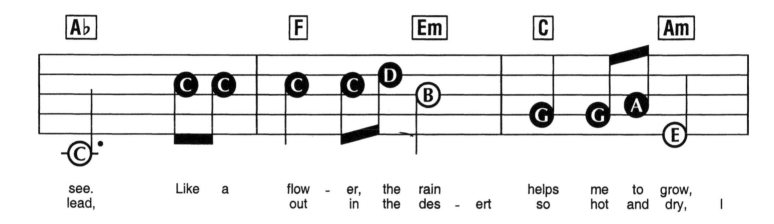

see.   Like   a   flow - er,   the   rain   helps   me   to   grow,
lead,   out   in   the   des - ert   so   hot   and   dry,   I

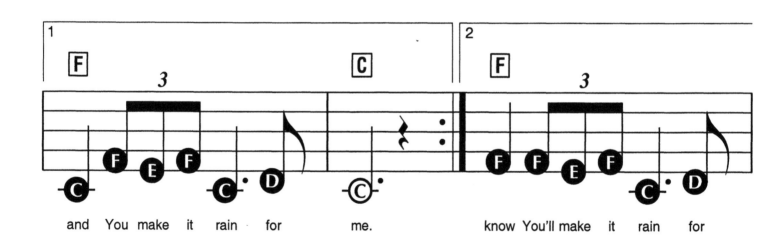

and   You   make   it   rain   for   me.
know You'll make   it   rain   for

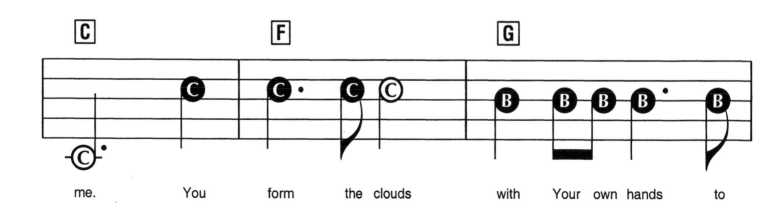

me.   You   form   the   clouds   with   Your   own   hands   to

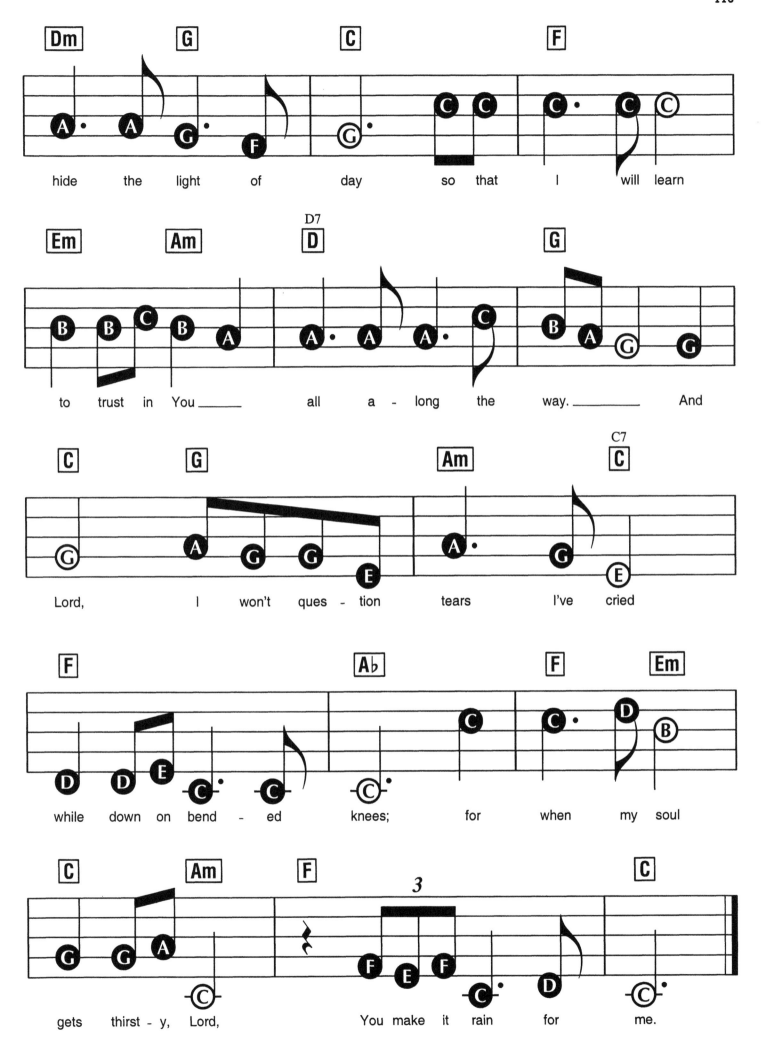

Registration Guide

- Match the Registration number on the song to the corresponding numbered category below. Select and activate an instrumental sound available on your instrument.

- Choose an automatic rhythm appropriate to the mood and style of the song. (Consult your Owner's Guide for proper operation of automatic rhythm features.)

- Adjust the tempo and volume controls to comfortable settings.

Registration

1	Mellow	Flutes, Clarinet, Oboe, Flugel Horn, Trombone, French Horn, Organ Flutes
2	Ensemble	Brass Section, Sax Section, Wind Ensemble, Full Organ, Theater Organ
3	Strings	Violin, Viola, Cello, Fiddle, String Ensemble, Pizzicato, Organ Strings
4	Guitars	Acoustic/Electric Guitars, Banjo, Mandolin, Dulcimer, Ukulele, Hawaiian Guitar
5	Mallets	Vibraphone, Marimba, Xylophone, Steel Drums, Bells, Celesta, Chimes
6	Liturgical	Pipe Organ, Hand Bells, Vocal Ensemble, Choir, Organ Flutes
7	Bright	Saxophones, Trumpet, Mute Trumpet, Synth Leads, Jazz/Gospel Organs
8	Piano	Piano, Electric Piano, Honky Tonk Piano, Harpsichord, Clavi
9	Novelty	Melodic Percussion, Wah Trumpet, Synth, Whistle, Kazoo, Perc. Organ
10	Bellows	Accordion, French Accordion, Mussette, Harmonica, Pump Organ, Bagpipes